SELECT LAB

PROJECTS FOR THE INTERNET

Linda Ericksen
Lane Community College
Emily Kim

▲ ADDISON-WESLEY

An imprint of Addison Wesley Longman, Inc.

Reading, Massachusetts • Menlo Park, California • New York • Harlow, England
Don Mills, Ontario • Sydney • Mexico City • Madrid • Amsterdam

Senior Editor: Carol Crowell
Production Supervision: Juliet Silveri
Copyeditor: Chuck Hutchinson
Proofreader: Cynthia Benn
Technical Editor: Pauline Johnson/Jennifer Annis/Lorilee Sadler
Indexer: Bernice Eisen
Composition: Compset, Inc.
Cover Design Supervisor: Gina Hagen
Marketing Manager: Michelle Hudson
Manufacturing Manager: Hugh Crawford

ISBN 0-201-31565-3

Ordering from the SELECT System
For more information on ordering and pricing policies for the SELECT Lab Series and supplements, please contact your Addison Wesley Longman sales representative or call 1-800-552-2499.

Addison-Wesley Publishing Company
One Jacob Way
Reading, MA 01867
http://hepg.awl.com/select/
is@awl.com

3 4 5 6 7 8 9 10-DOW-0099

This book is dedicated to my parents.

E. B. K.

This book is dedicated to all my students,
who have helped me become a better communicator
and a better human being.

L. E.

Preface to the Instructor

Welcome to the *SELECT Lab Series*. This applications series is designed specifically to make learning easy and enjoyable, a natural outcome of thoughtful, meaningful activity. The goal for the series is to create a learning environment in which students can explore the essentials of software applications, use critical thinking, and gain confidence and proficiency.

Greater access to ideas and information is changing the way people work. With today's business and communication application software, you have greater integration capabilities and easier access to Internet resources than ever before. The *SELECT Lab Series* helps you take advantage of these valuable resources, with special assignments devoted to the Internet and with additional connectivity resources that can be accessed through our Web site, **http://hepg.awl.com/select/.**

The *SELECT Lab Series* offers dozens of proven and class-tested materials, from the latest operating systems and browsers, to the most popular applications software for word processing, spreadsheets, databases, presentation graphics, desktop publishing, and integrated packages, to HTML, to programming. For your lab course, you can choose what you want to combine; your choice of lab manuals will be sent to the bookstore, combined in a TechSuite, allowing students to purchase all books in one convenient package at a discount.

The most popular *SELECT Lab Series* titles are available in three levels of coverage. The *SELECT Brief* features four projects that quickly lay the foundation of an application in three to five contact hours. The *standard edition SELECT* expands on material covered in the brief edition with five to eight projects that teach intermediate skills in just six to nine contact hours. *SELECT Plus* provides 10 to 12 projects that cover intermediate to advanced material in 12 to 14 contact hours.

Your Addison Wesley Longman representative will be happy to work with you and your bookstore manager to provide the most current menu of *SELECT Lab Series* offerings, outline the ordering process, and provide pricing, ISBNs, and delivery information. Or call 1-800-447-2226 or visit our Web site at http://www.awl.com/.

Organization

The "Overview of Windows 95", which is included in some *SELECT* modules, familiarizes students with Windows 95 before launching into the application. Students learn the basics of starting Windows 95, using a mouse, using the essential features of Windows 95, getting help, and exiting Windows 95.

An overview introduces the basic concepts of the application or browser and provides hands-on instructions to put students to work using the software immediately. Students learn problem-solving techniques while working through projects that provide practical, real-life scenarios that they can relate to.

Web assignments appear throughout the text at the end of each project, giving students practice using the Internet.

Approach

The *SELECT Lab Series* uses a document-centered approach to learning. Each project begins with a list of measurable objectives, a realistic scenario called the Challenge, a well-defined plan called the Solution, and an illustration of the final product. The Setup enables students to verify that the settings on the computer match those needed for the project. The project is arranged in carefully divided, highly visual objective-based tasks that foster confidence and self-reliance. Each project closes with a wrap-up of the project called the Conclusion, followed by summary questions, exercises, and assignments geared to reinforcing the information taught through the project.

Other Features

In addition to the document-centered, visual approach of each project, this book contains the following features:

- An overview so that students feel comfortable and confident as they function in the working environment.
- Keycaps and toolbar button icons within each step so that the student can quickly perform the required action.
- A comprehensive and well-organized end-of-the-project Summary and Exercises section for reviewing, integrating, and applying new skills.
- An illustration or description of the results of each step so that students know they're on the right track all the time.

1 PROJECT

Getting Online

In this project, you will learn the basics about how modems work and what to look for when buying a modem. You will also be presented with descriptions of the *online service providers* (OSPs) and the national, regional, and local *Internet service providers* (ISPs). Using the information in this project, you will be able to choose the Internet access provider that best suits your personal or business use.

Objectives

After completing this project, you will be able to do the following:

➤ Evaluate modems
➤ Describe the physical setup of the Internet
➤ Distinguish between the different service providers
➤ Choose the service provider that best fits your needs

The Challenge

Your employer has heard about the Internet and she's eager to get connected. She's given you the complete Internet project to manage. Your first step will be to evaluate modems. Then you will research Internet access providers and find the provider that best meets the needs of your organization, Wildlife Rescue International (WRI).

The Solution

In this project, you will learn how to get connected to the Internet and choose the Internet access provider that best meets the needs of your company, Wildlife Rescue International.

INET-16

The **Introduction** sets up the real-world scenario that serves as the environment for learning.

Clearly defined and measurable **objectives** give students the direction and focus they need to learn new material.

The **Challenge** introduces the goal of the project, the document, spreadsheet, database, or presentation to be created.

The **Solution** describes the plan for completing the projects, the tasks leading to the final product.

Clearly defined **tasks** guide students step by step through each process, providing reassurance and increasing confidence for independent or group work.

Appropriate, full-color illustrations shift the emphasis from text and toward the visual-based applications.

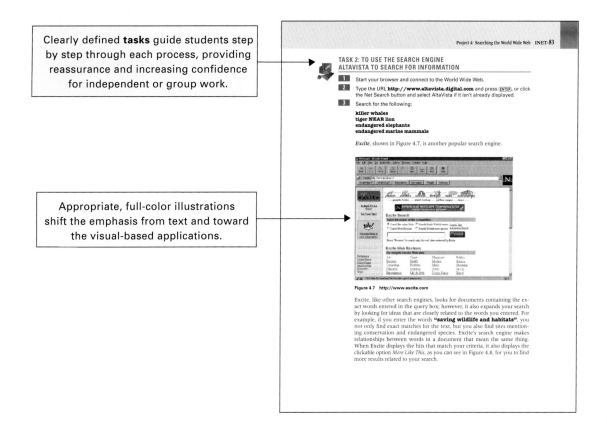

Project 4: Searching the World Wide Web   INET-83

TASK 2: TO USE THE SEARCH ENGINE ALTAVISTA TO SEARCH FOR INFORMATION

1 Start your browser and connect to the World Wide Web.

2 Type the URL **http://www.altavista.digital.com** and press ENTER, or click the Net Search button and select AltaVista if it isn't already displayed.

3 Search for the following:

killer whales
tiger NEAR lion
endangered elephants
endangered marine mammals

Excite, shown in Figure 4.7, is another popular search engine.

Figure 4.7   http://www.excite.com

Excite, like other search engines, looks for documents containing the exact words entered in the query box; however, it also expands your search by looking for ideas that are closely related to the words you entered. For example, if you enter the words **"saving wildlife and habitats"**, you not only find exact matches for the text, but you also find sites mentioning conservation and endangered species. Excite's search engine makes relationships between words in a document that mean the same thing. When Excite displays the hits that match your criteria, it also displays the clickable option *More Like This*, as you can see in Figure 4.8, for you to find more results related to your search.

---

keyword only in the body of the document. Also, if you're searching for multiple keywords, documents that contain all the keywords are ranked higher than documents that contain only some of the keywords.

 Tip Each search tool contains online help to help you narrow your search.

To help you narrow your directory search in Yahoo!, use the following tips:

* Use double quotation marks around words that should be considered a phrase. For example, by placing quotation marks around **"Pacific Humpback whales"**, you find only results that match the words in the exact sequence.
* Place a plus sign in front of words that must be found in every search result. Placing a plus sign in front of *tiger* in **+Siberian+Tiger** requires that the word *tiger* be found in all results; therefore, you don't get *Siberian Husky* matches.
* Place a minus sign in front of words that must not be found in your search results. Placing a minus sign in front of *island* in **+Kodiak+bear-island** requires that search results containing the words *Kodiak Island* would not appear in the resulting list of matches.

 Tip When typing in text to search for, don't include spaces between the words if you are including an operator such as the plus sign (+), and be careful of making words plural because it will result in the word only appearing as plural in the hits.

The results of searches are called *hits*. You can see the total number of hits that resulted, but usually only the first 10 or 20 hits are displayed along with a brief description of the site. If more hits result, you can click on an option to display the next group of results if you don't find what you want in the first group. The list of results contains hyperlinks to corresponding sites, so you can simply click the link to be transferred to a site.

TASK 1: TO USE THE DIRECTORY YAHOO! TO SEARCH FOR INFORMATION

1 Start your browser and connect to the World Wide Web.

2 Type the URL **http://www.yahoo.com** and press (ENTER), or click the Net Search button and select Yahoo! if it isn't already displayed.

3 Use the directories and keyword searches to help Wildlife Rescue International locate information on the following topics:

Kenya's black rhinoceros
Galapagos Islands
whooping cranes
scarlet macaws
lowland gorillas

Tips, Reminders, Cautions, and Troubleshooting sections appear at appropriate spots throughout each project to highlight important, helpful, or pertinent information.

Each topic begins with a brief introductory paragraph that explains the concepts and operations students will learn.

Managing E-mail

This section will review some of the more advanced features in e-mail programs that help you organize your messages. General explanations of the features are given here, and features in several e-mail programs are reviewed later in this project.

Filters

Filters are a handy feature for people who get a lot of e-mail messages. Most filters use the information in the headers of e-mail messages to sort through mail.

For example, you may receive a lot of e-mail jokes from your friend Patsy who works for IBM. Because you don't always have time to read these messages immediately, you can have all messages with the e-mail address patsy@ibm.com in the FROM: section of the header put into a different folder that you can read through later, as shown in Figure 2.7. This way, you can free up space in the e-mail *inbox* for messages that require immediate attention. The inbox is where messages first enter your program. They wait there to be read or processed by features like filters.

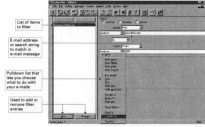

List of items to filter

E-mail address or search string to match in e-mail message

Pulldown list that lets you choose what to do with your e-mails

Used to add or remove filter entries

Figure 2.7

With more advanced software, you can sort through messages by filtering information that's not only in the headers of the e-mail messages, but also in the body of the messages.

---

6 Make sure you fully investigate any res For example, after you ask for a dial-up times during the day to check whether

7 After you complete your investigation, **an Internet Access Provider - After (** document.

8 Summarize your impressions of the acc you would still consider using it and wh

9 Save your work, and close the word pro

Conclusion

Now that you've completed Project 1 mary, and do the following exercises.

Each project ends with **The Conclusion**, a concise paragraph that wraps up the loose ends and enables the student to present a final, completed project for evaluation.

A bulleted **summary list** further reinforces the objectives and the material presented in the project.

Key Terms are boldface and italicized throughout each project and then listed for handy review in the summary section at the end of the project.

Twenty-four **study questions** (Multiple Choice, Short Answer, and For Discussion) bring the content of the project into focus again and allow for independent or group review of the material learned.

Assignments invoke critical thinking and encourage integration of project skills.

Review Exercises present hands-on tasks for building on the skills acquired in the project.

Summary and Exercises

Summary

- Internet directories are catalogs of Web sites compiled by researchers, who include only relevant sites and often rate sites for their relevance to your search.
- Keywords, which you type in the query box, are the words that the search tool matches in the database
- The results of searches are called hits.
- Search engines search for the keyword or words you type into the query box and find documents that contain the words.
- Search engines use software called spiders, webcrawlers, or robots that compile databases.
- Boolean logic developed by George Boole, a nineteenth-century mathematician, applies mathematical symbols to logic to help clarify and simplify logical relationships.
- Specialized directories serve specific searching needs such as finding e-mail addresses, phone numbers, street addresses, and information on businesses and government agencies.
- Cookies are text files that Web sites you visit store on your computer.

Key Terms

AltaVista	Lycos
BigBook	Metacrawler
Bigfoot	meta search tools
Boolean logic	robots
cookies	search engines
directories	search tool
Excite	snail mail
Four11	spiders
hits	query box
HotBot	WebCrawler
index	webcrawlers
Infoseek	WhoWhere?
keywords	Yahoo!

Study Questions

Multiple Choice
1. A directory
   a. is compiled by a robot.
   b. makes use of spider programs.
   c. is compiled by a human.
   d. is also known as a spelling checker.
   e. is useful if you aren't sure what information you're looking for.

INET-91

INET-34

Assignments

1. Getting Connected
In this project, you learned about modems and [...] mation in this project to rate your personal [...] your ideal modem. Use speed, features, and c[...] rating. Write a brief description of your modem[...]

2. Using a Personal Internet Account
In this project, you learned how to find the bes[...] account. Use the information that you learned [...] match for your own personal Internet access a[...] line services (such as AOL and CompuServe), [...] cess accounts (such as AT&T, IBM, and MCI), a[...] town's local nonprofit Internet access organiza[...] service providers in your area, write an evalua[...]

What Does It Cost?

Excerpt from an article by Robin Frost. Reprinted by pe[...] cember 9, 1996, copyright 1996 Dow Jones & Company,

How much does it cost to go on-line?
If you're just getting started in cyberspace and already have a PC, it seems like an easy question: a hundred dollars or so for a modem, maybe $20 a month for a service provider, and that's that.
But the price question is actually more complicated. There are hardware decisions to make long before you get a modem that will affect your bill considerably. Service providers vary widely in the prices—and options—they offer. After you have chosen a service, there are still more charges that can crop up.
So, to help you along, here's a look at exactly how much it will cost you to catch the wave in cyberspace.
To begin with, there's the seemingly obvious question of what kind of computer you need. The question to ask yourself: Just how detailed do you want your cruises through cyberspace to be?
The old 486 machine lurking on the desktop is fine if all you're interested in is reading newsgroups on the Internet or traveling to text-heavy World Wide Web sites; even a creaky 386 is fine for downloading e-mail. But if you want to experience all the bells and whistles on the Web—file and music clips, 3-D sites, animation—you're going to have to make big investments in new hardware.
The key word to buying a computer for high-level surfing: multimedia. You'll need a good graphics card and sound card—pieces of hardware that let your computer show pictures or play sounds—stereo speakers, a huge hard drive (one or two gigabytes), 32 megabytes of memory and at least a four-speed CD-ROM drive. (Why the CD-ROM? Some disks let you update their software by accessing a Web site.) For PC users, it is advisable to go with Microsoft Corp.'s Windows '95 operating system; many Web software applications require it. This package should set you back $2,000 to $3,000.
Another key word is speed. Your machine's processor chip should be fast—at least 120 megahertz, and faster won't hurt given the rapid evolution of Internet applications. A 14.4-kilobit-per-second modem, usually the basic speed, costs under $100, and is fine for rifling newsgroups or even browsing, if you don't mind waiting a couple of minutes for graphics-heavy pages to download. If you want to keep the Web animation fairly brisk and downloads as short as possible, get the current standard for most companies—a 28.8 modem. It will cost under $200. For the fastest standard modems, some companies are offering 33.6-kbps models for $200 to $300.

---

   d. the Microsoft Network.
   e. none of the above.

10. Redundancy
   a. causes breaks in Internet connectivity.
   b. causes a slowdown in transmission speed.
   c. helps stabilize the network.
   d. clears up noise coming over a modem.
   e. is required of online service providers.

Short Answer
1. Define ISP.
2. Outline how a modem works.
3. Define bps.
4. Name the V-dot standard for error correction.
5. What is the criterion to be a backbone operator?
6. What advantages do OSPs and national and regional ISPs have for travelers?
7. PCMCIA creates the standards for what system?
8. Name the four major OSPs.
9. Define set-top system.
10. A T3 line transfers data at what speed?

For Discussion
1. Discuss the advantages and disadvantages of using an online service such as AOL or CompuServe for your Internet access.
2. Discuss why you might choose a regional ISP for your Internet access.
3. Discuss the pros and cons of using a company such as AT&T for your Internet access.
4. What advantages do set-top systems have over regular computer systems?
5. Explain why the selection of your Internet access provider is an important decision.

Review Exercises

1. Investigating Online Services
Use magazine reviews, interview subscribers, or log on to one of the four large online services—Prodigy, CompuServe, America Online, and the Microsoft Network—to evaluate their ease of use, availability of help, services, customer support, and ease of canceling a subscription. You can go to their respective Web sites to download a free trial version of their software or use one of the many disks that come in computer magazines.

2. Examining FreeNets
In many communities, nonprofit corporations or libraries use FreeNets. Check for one in your area, and if you cannot find a FreeNet there, find the closest one. Gather information about the FreeNet, and write a paper using the research to tell how it works, who runs it, what it costs, and what is provided.

Supplements

You get extra support for this text from supplemental materials, including the *Instructor's Manual* and the Instructor's Data Disk.

The *Instructor's Manual* includes a Test Bank for each project in the student text, Expanded Student Objectives, Answers to Study Questions, and Additional Assessment Techniques. The Test Bank contains two separate tests with answers and consists of multiple-choice, true/false, and fill-in questions referenced to pages in the student text. Transparency Masters illustrate key concepts and screen captures from the text.

The Instructor's Data Disk contains student data files, completed data files for Review Exercises and assignments, and the test files from the *Instructor's Manual* in ASCII format.

See the SELECT web site for supplementary materials for Internet and browser-related lab manuals.

About the Authors

Linda Ericksen teaches in the Department of Business Technologies at Lane Community College, Eugene, Oregon. She is the author of 12 computer text books, including *Projects for HTML*, also in the *SELECT* series. She also conducts workshops for government agencies and for businesses. She has an MS degree in Computer Science/Education and an MA degree in English. Linda is the current President of the Oregon Chapter of the American Association of Women in Community Colleges and serves on the Technology Advising and Coordinating Team for Lane Community College.

Emily Kim received a bachelor's degree from the University of California, Davis in 1994. After graduation, she worked at UC Davis for two years as a Computer Resource Specialist. She maintained computer hardware, provided software support, taught Internet awareness, and designed the departmental World Wide Web site and various teaching manuals. In 1995, she started Paper Tiger, an Internet consulting business. In addition to creating and maintaining World Wide Web sites for businesses in California and Colorado, she has been the technical and developmental consultant on several Internet books. She would be happy to hear from you and can be reached by e-mail at emily@paper-tiger.com.

Thanks to . . .

Without a doubt, I could never have written this book without the support of my friends and relatives — I thank you all from the bottom of my heart. There are three people who I especially need to thank: Mark Hoggard who has the patience of a god and who always has time for just one more dumb question; Barb Terry for her great ideas and for just being her wonderful self; and of course, Linda Ericksen for thinking of me and being my better half for six months . . . oh yeah, and yes, thanks to even YOU, Michael, for supporting me, criticizing my grammar, and pretending to read my manuscript even when you could barely keep your eyes open:)

E. B. K.

I would like to thank Carol Crowell, Senior Editor, for her continued support of my writing efforts. I also want to thank Emily Kim for her hard work, without which this book would not be a reality.

L. E.

Acknowledgments

Addison-Wesley Publishing Company would like to thank the following reviewers for their valuable contributions to the *SELECT Lab Series*.

James Agnew
Northern Virginia
Community College

Joseph Aieta
Babson College

Dr. Muzaffar Ali
Bellarmine College

Tom Ashby
Oklahoma CC

Bob Barber
Lane CC

Robert Caruso
Santa Rosa Junior
College

Robert Chi
California State
Long Beach

Jill Davis
State University of New
York at Stony Brook

Fredia Dillard
Samford University

Peter Drexel
Plymouth State College

David Egle
University of Texas, Pan
American

Linda Ericksen
Lane Community College

Jonathan Frank
Suffolk University

Patrick Gilbert
University of Hawaii

Maureen Greenbaum
Union County College

Sally Ann Hanson
Mercer County CC

Sunil Hazari
East Carolina University

Gloria Henderson
Victor Valley College

Bruce Herniter
University of Hartford

Rick Homkes
Purdue University

Lisa Jackson
Henderson CC

Martha Johnson
(technical reviewer)
Delta State University

Cynthia Kachik
Santa Fe CC

Bennett Kramer
Massasoit CC

Charles Lake
Faulkner State Junior
College

Ron Leake
Johnson County CC

Randy Marak
Hill College

Charles Mattox, Jr.
St. Mary's University

Jim McCullough
Porter and Chester
Institute

Gail Miles
Lenoir-Rhyne College

Steve Moore
University of South
Florida

Anthony Nowakowski
Buffalo State College

Gloria Oman
Portland State University

John Passafiume
Clemson University

Leonard Presby
William Paterson
College

Louis Pryor
Garland County CC

Michael Reilly
University of Denver

Dick Ricketts
Lane CC

Dennis Santomauro
Kean College of
New Jersey

Pamela Schmidt
Oakton CC

Gary Schubert
Alderson-Broaddus
College

T. Michael Smith
Austin CC

Cynthia Thompson
Carl Sandburg College

Marion Tucker
Northern Oklahoma
College

JoAnn Weatherwax
Saddleback College

David Whitney
San Francisco State
University

James Wood
Tri-County Technical
College

Minnie Yen
University of Alaska,
Anchorage

Allen Zilbert
Long Island University

Contents

Overview

Most everyone has heard of the Internet, the Information Superhighway, the Web, the Net, WWW, or any of the multitude of terms that refer to the network of computers spanning the globe. In this overview, you will become familiar with how the Internet works, where it came from, and what it is composed of. In later projects, you will use various aspects of the Internet.

Objectives

After completing this overview, you will be able to do the following:

➤ **Understand the history of the Internet**

➤ **Describe cyberspace and what it offers**

➤ **Describe social issues related to the Internet**

➤ **Describe a typical Internet session**

A Historical Look at the Internet

In 1957 at the height of the Cold War, the USSR (the former Soviet Union) launched the satellite Sputnik, and President Dwight Eisenhower set up the Advanced Research Projects Agency (ARPA) so that the USSR would not take the lead in the space race. Over the next few years, ARPA started researching computer communications, and in 1969 the U.S. Department of Defense (DOD) established the Advanced Research Projects Agency Network (otherwise known as *ARPAnet*), linking four universities together—University of California–Los Angeles, Stanford Research Institute, University of California–Santa Barbara, and the University of Utah.

The DOD's goal was to create a communications link that could withstand disaster—such as a nuclear attack. If the communications network depended on one central computer, then all communications could be knocked out by one missile. Instead, the ARPAnet model was decentralized, with messages traveling from a source to a destination rather than to a main computer.

During the 1970s, ARPAnet expanded and other networks were also established at universities. In the late 1970s, Usenet, which stores news articles and categorizes them into **newsgroups**, or computerized discussion groups, was established. Reading research articles and communicating by electronic mail (**e-mail**) became an everyday practice for researchers at many universities.

In the early 1980s, a communication **protocol**, or standard, known as Transmission Control Protocol/Internet Protocol (or more commonly called **TCP/IP**) was made available, and this advance provided the means for the development of the Internet.

Computer networks linked to the Internet make use of the TCP/IP protocol, which allows computers to communicate. The communication is based on **packet switching**, which is actually a simple concept. Each message is broken down into parts called **packets**. These packets that contain the address of the recipient and the sender travel the Internet separately over different paths and are reassembled by the recipient's computer. If a packet is lost or becomes garbled, then the recipient's computer asks for that packet to be re-sent. This concept can be likened to sending a 10-page report by placing each page in a separate envelope. The outside of the envelope contains the sender's address, the recipient's address, and the page number of the page inside; furthermore, the envelope must be addressed in a way that can be read by any computer that it encounters on the way. TCP (Transmission Control Protocol) is the packet standard, and IP (Internet Protocol) is the addressing standard.

Internet addresses (IPs) are composed of four groups of numbers that are separated by periods. These numbers represent the address of the **domain** (a series of computers that are grouped together) and the address of the host computer that should receive the message. A typical Internet address looks like this: 121.115.19.3. The IP address supplies information to computers called **routers**, which read the address and send the packet on the right course. Figure O.1 illustrates this process.

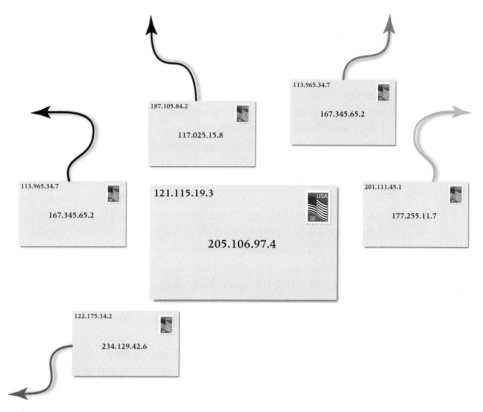

Figure O.1

A packet-switched network provides several important advantages. First, if part of the network is down, the packets all contain the address of the recipient and can travel different routes to the destination. Second, no single message ties up the network; small packets are routed over different communication lines. Third, packets can be encrypted for privacy. Fourth, each packet contains the result of a mathematical formula. The receiving computer quickly performs a calculation known as a **checksum**—a mathematical calculation performed by both computers which must result in the same answer. If the answer does not match the result in the packet, then the data was garbled, and the recipient asks the sender to send that particular packet again. This process speeds up communication because only the parts of the message that have become corrupted must be retransmitted.

During the 1980s, technical advances helped set the stage for the Internet's future growth. The first advancement was to replace the old communications model known as **host–remote**. In this relationship, the remote computer, on your desktop, is either a dumb terminal or a personal computer that emulates a dumb terminal (has no processing power of its own); all the processing of information takes place on the host computer, and the remote computer simply receives the information. A new communications model known as *client–server* enabled communication between the client, on your desktop, and a server, which is a more powerful computer. This model allows the client to communicate with other computers and at the same time make use of its own processing power.

Second, computers in government agencies, universities, and corporations became networked to each other locally as local area networks (or LANs). With these networks, employees could share data, provide intraorganizational e-mail, and share expensive peripherals, such as laser printers. These networks were ready for the next advance, needing only a *gateway,* or computer that provides Internet access.

Another advance that took place in the 1980s was the development of the text transfer protocol called *Gopher,* which was developed at the University of Minnesota. Gopher provided a way to find information on the Internet. Gopher helped bring the Internet to people who had no background working in the UNIX operating system used by most computers connected to the Internet. People who did not have technical, computer backgrounds found UNIX difficult to use, so the introduction of Gopher set the stage for the development of friendly Internet tools and also helped people see the usefulness of computer searches.

In 1986, the National Science Foundation (NSF) developed a network (*NSFNet*) that connected supercomputer centers, research institutes, and schools and universities, making electronic communication a part of everyday life on campus. This network became the *backbone,* or infrastructure, of the Internet. This advancement allowed several host computers to be grouped together into **domains**, or groups. The domains could then be connected to the Internet, as illustrated in Figure O.2.

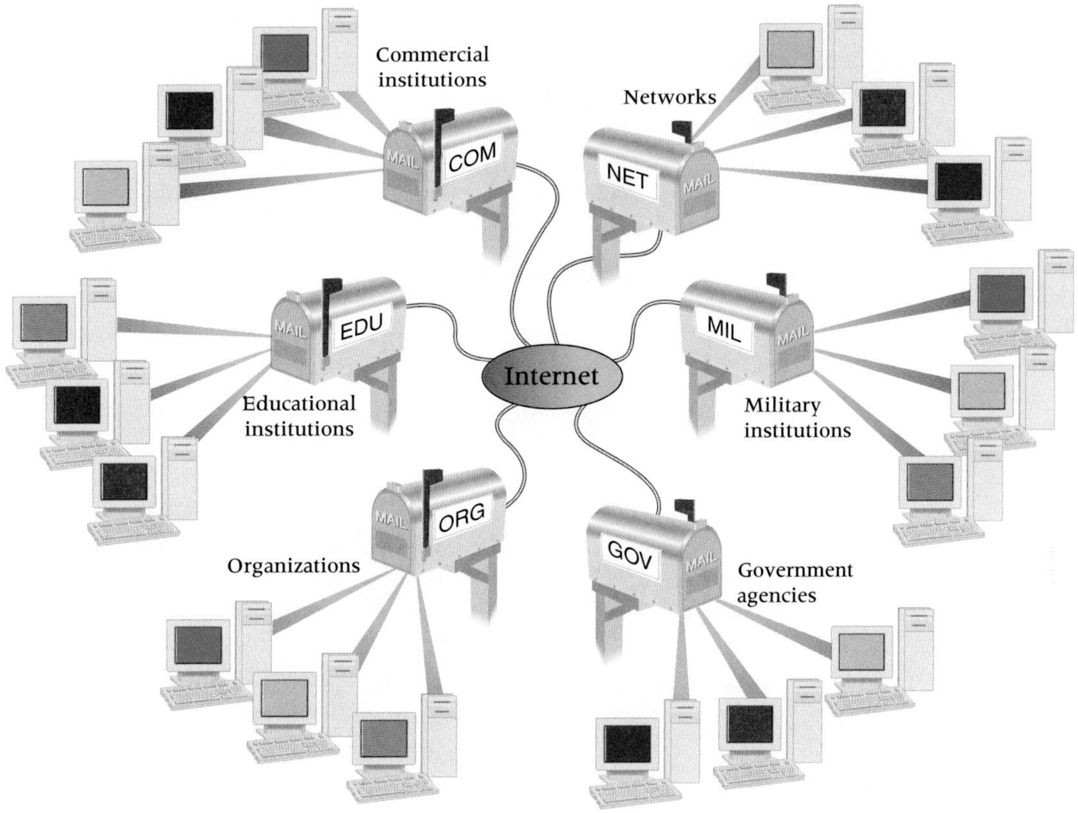

Figure O.2

Also in the 1980s, people began to use personal computers to communicate with **electronic bulletin board systems** (BBSs) and to communicate with others via e-mail. For a fee, computer users could subscribe to services such as Prodigy or CompuServe, two of the first electronic service providers available outside the academic environment. These new technologies helped bring the idea of online communication to personal computer users.

Many dramatic advances took place in the 1990s, making the Internet important to all computer users. ARPAnet ceased to exist in 1990. The National Science Foundation stopped funding the backbone network in 1995, thus making the Internet a commercial venture. In 1992, the **World Wide Web (WWW)** was made available. It was developed in 1989 by Tim Berners-Lee at CERN, the European Laboratory for Particle Physics in Geneva, Switzerland.

The World Wide Web is a collection of documents that are linked together by **hyperlinks**. When you click on a hypertext or "hot" word, you are linked to a related document. Figure O.3 shows a Web page with hyper-links.

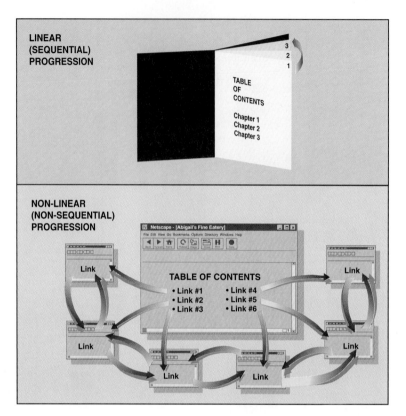

Figure O.3

In 1993, the National Center for Superconducting Applications (NCSA) released Mosaic, developed by Marc Andreessen and others at the University of Illinois at Champaign-Urbana. Mosaic was the first graphical Web *browser*, an easy-to-use piece of software that allows you to click the mouse not only on text but also on graphics or icons to link to a document in another location. Marc Andreessen and others went on to form a private company, Netscape Communications Corporation, that markets software to browse the Web. This software is known as Netscape Navigator.

Information on every imaginable topic is now available on the World Wide Web. You can *surf* the Web—finding new information, looking at "cool" sites, performing serious research, or conducting business. You also can contact government officials, plan vacations, find other people with like interests, or simply find out new information. *Hypermedia* has become available in the new wave of browsers, providing not only text and graphics but also multimedia.

The 1992 Clinton/Gore presidential campaign brought the notion of an *information superhighway* to the people of the United States. The campaign called for a *National Information Infrastructure* that would link computers, telephones, and television and be affordable for everyone. After winning their first election, President Bill Clinton and Vice President Al Gore brought the White House online. You can reach them by e-mail at the following addresses:

President Clinton: president@whitehouse.gov
Vice-President Gore: vice-president@whitehouse.gov

You also can "visit" the White House by pointing your browser to http:// www.whitehouse.gov/.

The Internet has become the communications phenomenon of the late twentieth century, with many historians and educators likening it to the creation of the printing press because of the social, economic, and political changes it has initiated.

What Is Cyberspace and Why Would You Go There?

The word *cyberspace* was first used in the 1984 science fiction novel *Neuromancer* by William Gibson to describe the place beyond the computer that is real even if you can't actually see it. Today, this term is used to describe the communications that take place on the Internet; it is also used to describe many aspects of the Internet such as cyberdating, cybermalls, cybergambling, and so on.

People who are new to the Internet, often called *newbies*, wonder who controls it and who pays for it. No single body has control over the Internet; however, the networks that connect to the Internet are controlled by their organizations and can charge for use. Because much of the infrastructure was developed by government agencies, taxpayers have paid a share in its development and continued use.

People surf the Net (short for the Internet) for a variety of reasons. Some do research, and others use it as a form of entertainment and even shopping, whereas others form relationships with people who share like interests. Sociologists have coined the name *Virtual Communities* for groups of people who come together through the Internet. These people have common interests, share communication, and feel a sense of community with others who are online. One phenomenon that has grown out of people communicating online is cyberdating. The Net has evolved from sharing scientific data to providing a means to meet others romantically. Many news stories tell of people who met online and later met FTF (face-to-face) and married. Other news stories detail the dangers of people who create online personas to attract naïve users into dangerous relationships.

Cybermalls have sprung up all over the Net, allowing people to shop from home. These shopping malls will gain in popularity as security measures allow for safe transfer of credit card information over the Internet. Another feature, Cybergambling, is available for those who want to enter virtual casinos to gamble or simply bet on their favorite sports teams.

Social Issues Involving the Internet

The social impact of the Internet is ever present in your everyday life. Some of this impact is positive, but some is not.

For example, some people are addicted to being online. Research into Internet Addiction Disorder has brought about help for companies whose productivity has declined because of employee addiction and for individuals whose relationships offline are suffering. As more enticing multimedia sites are available and more people use the Internet, addiction could become a major economic and social issue.

Another impact of the Internet is the loss of privacy for everyone. As every site you visit on the Internet records your address, a profile of your cyberidentity emerges. This recording of information is used to market products that are of interest to you, and will help you find other related information based on information you have already sought. However nice these advantages sound, the reality of others compiling a user profile that may or may not be accurate feels like an invasion of privacy to many people.

Another issue that has received extensive coverage in recent years is the question of whether the Internet is safe for children. Because some adult sites feature cyberporn, parents and schools want to ensure that their children are not exposed to pornography. Newer browsers allow parents to block or erase objectionable Web sites. These concerns for the safety of children using the Internet led to the passage of the U.S. Communications Decency Act in 1996. This law prohibits distribution of indecent materials over the Net, but it is controversial for many people who feel the government is taking control of the Net. The law has never been enforced because an injunction was placed on its enforcement.

Social issues such as Internet access for all people—despite income, gender, or race—are also becoming important. (See the Info Box at the end of this Overview for statistics on who is using the Internet.) Market predictions indicate that needing an expensive personal computer with a modem to have access to the Internet will soon be unnecessary. New advances—such as WebTV and Network Computers—will reduce the hardware investment to less than $300, connecting a television and an existing phone line to access the Internet. However, this amount will still be beyond the means of some people.

Forecasters predict that in the year 2000 approximately 200 million people around the world will have Internet access. International borders, political affiliations, time zones, and other barriers can become insignificant when people around the world communicate with each other. If, however, governments restrict access, control content, and invade citizens' privacy, users will not feel free to communicate openly on the Net.

What Happens When You Log On the Internet?

To use the Internet, your computer must have a connection. In a business or college where computers are networked together, the network generally has a gateway computer that provides Internet access.

If you have a stand-alone computer in your home, the computer must have a modem and be connected to a phone line. A modem is a device that converts the digital signal—discrete on and off switches of the computer—and modulates them so that they can travel through the phone lines. The receiving computer also has a modem that demodulates the signal so that it can be understood by that computer.

Once you have the hardware in place, you need to have access to an Internet service provider (ISP) or be connected to a computer service such as America Online (AOL), Microsoft Network (MSN), or others that provide Internet access. The ISP provides accounts for a monthly fee, which can vary in price and services. The two most common types of accounts are Serial Line Internet Protocol (SLIP) and the newer Point-to-Point Protocol (PPP). With these protocols, your modem can interact with IP, the Internet Protocol.

After you establish an account with an ISP, and you have a *UserID*, which is the name you use to log on to the Internet, you need to choose a *password*, which is a special code word you use to identify yourself. Passwords provide a significant defense against illegal computer logins, but most people simply use the names of their dogs or simple words found in the dictionary. Because *hackers* who want to break in to computers have developed programs that run continuously trying different passwords, choosing a password that is not in the dictionary is best. If you do use a real word, then you should embed a number in the word.

Having completed the preceding steps, you can dial the number of your Internet service provider. Most software that provides Internet access can be configured to maintain the main phone number and a secondary number of the ISP, so you don't actually dial but instead click the appropriate icon. Most software maintains your UserID and even your password; if it doesn't, you are asked to type in this information. ISPs usually have racks of modems that receive your incoming call and software that matches your UserID and password to make sure that you're using a legal account. After the connection is established, the ISP connects you to the Internet backbone by means of a T1 or T3 leased phone line (very fast lines dedicated only to Internet connections). Now you can browse the Web, check your e-mail, download software or files, or chat with others online. (You will learn to do all these tasks and more in the subsequent projects.) As you perform these activities, your requests for files are routed along the backbone to the appropriate computer. The transmission lines include telephone lines, fiber optic cables, microwave, and satellite links that carry messages at speeds up to 45 megabits per second (millions of bits per second)—and soon at speeds in the gigabytes (billions of bytes per second).

Earlier you saw that an IP or Internet address consisted of four sets of numbers separated by periods. Because some people think that numbers are too difficult to use, a naming system was developed to provide names. To provide unique names, the Network Information Center (NIC) set up a registry. One problem with the rapid growth of the Internet is that finding unused, meaningful names has become difficult. The Domain Name System was developed to organize names by their organization type. Domain names are words separated by periods; these words are then converted into their numeric IP by software. An example domain name is:

lanecc.or.edu

In this example, lanecc refers to the computers at Lane Community College. This name is followed by the group, or, which is educational computers in Oregon. The last name, edu, is the top-level domain name, that is, educational computers. Table O.1 lists six of the top-level domain names.

Table O.1

Domain Name	Type of Organization
edu	Educational institution
com	Commercial organization
gov	Government
mil	Military
org	Nonprofit organization
net	Networks

As the Internet becomes more international, the highest level domain name reflects the country of the computer. In the example www.silver-speed.com.au, the au tells you that the document is located on a server in Australia.

When you request a document located on another computer, a Domain Name Server (DNS) matches the domain name with the IP numeric address, and a router finds routes for the packets to travel. When the request is delivered, the receiving computer sends the requested files over the Internet in the same way.

If you find software on the Internet that you want to download to your computer, you should be aware of the danger of viruses. Hackers sometimes embed software with a virus that will spring into action when you use the software; this virus can damage your system. Before you download any software, you should back up your system and install a virus checker. Always make sure that software you download is from a reputable source with a name you can easily identify.

The Next Step

In the subsequent projects, I will introduce you to Wildlife Rescue International, a nonprofit corporation that is dedicated to preserving endangered species, helping injured animals, and providing educational activities. Wildlife Rescue International, which has a large international membership and maintains locations in various parts of the world, is about to use the Internet in its everyday business. You will help these folks to set up an Internet account and learn to use various features of the Internet.

Summary and Exercises

Summary

- The Department of Defense (DOD) established *ARPAnet* (Advanced Research Projects Agency Network), linking four universities together in 1969.
- Computer networks linked to the Internet make use of the TCP/IP protocol, which makes use of *packet switching*.
- Browsers enable you to display Web documents.
- The word *cyberspace* describes the place beyond the computer.
- Privacy, addiction, safety for children, and access for all people are some of the social issues raised by connecting to the Internet.
- You need a modem to connect a computer to a phone line.
- An Internet service provider, or ISP, provides accounts for people to access the Internet.
- The Domain Name System organizes networks under domains.

Key Terms

ARPAnet	hypermedia
backbone	information superhighway
browser	newbies
checksum	newsgroup
client–server	NSFNet
cyberspace	packet
domain	packet switching
e-mail	password
electronic bulletin board system	protocol
gateway	routers
Gopher	surf
hackers	TCP/IP
host–remote	UserID
hyperlinks	virtual communities
hypertext	World Wide Web

Study Questions

Multiple Choice

1. A protocol is
   a. a remote computer.
   b. a set of standards.
   c. a group of networks.
   d. hypermedia.
   e. all these answers.

2. The World Wide Web is
   a. a network of computer networks.
   b. a domain.
   c. a web of linked documents.
   d. primarily for military use.
   e. all these answers.

3. Packets
   a. contain the address of the sender.
   b. contain the address of the recipient.
   c. contain data.
   d. contain the checksum.
   e. all of these answers.

4. The first network that linked four universities was known as
   a. TCP/IP.
   b. NSFNet.
   c. BBS.
   d. ARPAnet.
   e. Gopher.

5. When you are on the Internet, you can
   a. send and receive e-mail.
   b. shop with your credit card.
   c. gamble.
   d. do research.
   e. all these answers.

6. An example of browser software is
   a. Gopher.
   b. ARPAnet.
   c. Netscape Navigator.
   d. hypertext.
   e. e-mail.

7. Packet-switching networks
   a. break messages up to be sent.
   b. allow messages to travel by different routes.
   c. allow for retransmission of only the garbled data.
   d. keep the network working fast.
   e. all these answers.

8. A modem
   a. modulates the outgoing message.
   b. demodulates the incoming message.
   c. is necessary on both ends of the communication.
   d. hooks to the phone line.
   e. all these answers.

9. TCP
   a. is the protocol that governs the packets.
   b. is the protocol that governs the Internet addresses.
   c. issues domain names.
   d. is the computer that routes the message.
   e. is a network.

10. IP
   a. is the protocol that governs the packets.
   b. is the protocol that governs the Internet addresses.
   c. issues domain names.
   d. is the computer that routes the message.
   e. is a network.

Short Answer

1. The top-level domain name in the address ca.efn.org is _____.

2. What is a protocol?

3. What is hypermedia?

4. What is a browser?

5. Describe the host–remote model.

6. What is cyberspace?

7. Describe packet switching.

8. What is the Internet backbone?

9. What is a newbie?

10. Describe the World Wide Web.

For Discussion

1. Describe the types of passwords that should be used.

2. Describe privacy issues on the Internet.

3. Discuss safety for children on the Internet.

4. Discuss access issues in regards to the Internet.

5. Discuss the issue of addiction in regards to the Internet.

Review Exercises

1. Creating a Timeline
Create a timeline showing the major advances in the history of the Internet.

2. Reading an Article and Writing a Summary
Read an article from a computer or Internet magazine on a social issue described in this Overview or another Internet issue that interests you. Write a one-page summary of the article.

Assignments

1. Determining Popular Uses of the Internet
Talk to at least five people you know who use the Internet to find out what they use it for most. Have them rank the aspects they use most. Write a one-page summary of your findings. Use your word processing software to create a chart of the most-used features.

2. Determining the Impact of the Internet on Business and Education
Talk to educators and business people to find out how the Internet has had an impact on their jobs. Ask them how it will affect them in the future. Write a one-page report of your findings.

Who Uses the Internet?

Everything you might guess about the typical World Wide Web user is true.

Yes, the Web user is more likely to be a man than a woman. Yes, the user is more likely to be young than old. Yes, the user is probably more educated and wealthier than the average person. And the user is probably in a professional or computer-related job.

But even though the stereotypes still hold, things are changing. The Web, which barely existed four years ago, shows clear signs of evolving into a mainstream medium. Just about everyone agrees that the average on-line user is getting less nerdy and more average.

Now more women are going on-line, say the myriad research firms that track Internet usage. And more of the households that own personal computers are venturing onto the Internet, potentially bringing entire families on-line.

That spells good news for businesses looking to tap the Internet as a marketing medium. It also means more options for individual users. As mainstream consumers flock to the Web in growing numbers, businesses hoping to sell them products and services will follow.

What no one knows for sure is how quickly this will take place. So far, the growth of the Internet user base has been nothing short of phenomenal. International Data Corp., a technology research firm in Framingham, Mass., says that the number of Web users world-wide will hit 35 million this month, about double the number a year ago. And the wider that universe grows, the more likely it is to reflect mainstream consumers.

But skeptics caution that continuation of this exponential growth is far from guaranteed. "We are going to see a slowdown in the rate of growth of on-line penetration," says J. Walker Smith, a partner at Yankelovich Partners, a market-research firm in Norwalk, Conn. "Online users are going to become a stable, identifiable group."

One simple fact supports Mr. Smith's contention: To get on the Web now, you need a computer and a modem. And while the ranks of users on-line have been growing like gangbusters, the growth in the number of homes with personal computers has slowed to only 7.6% this year—about a third of 1995's rate, according to Dataquest. Once the on-line market exhausts the pool of home-PC owners, mainstreaming could hit a wall.

PROJECT

Getting Online

In this project, you will learn the basics about how modems work and what to look for when buying a modem. You will also be presented with descriptions of the *online service providers* (OSPs) and the national, regional, and local *Internet service providers* (ISPs). Using the information in this project, you will be able to choose the Internet access provider that best suits your personal or business use.

Objectives

After completing this project, you will be able to do the following:

➤ **Evaluate modems**

➤ **Describe the physical setup of the Internet**

➤ **Distinguish between the different service providers**

➤ **Choose the service provider that best fits your needs**

The Challenge

Your employer has heard about the Internet and she's eager to get connected. She's given you the complete Internet project to manage. Your first step will be to evaluate modems. Then you will research Internet access providers and find the provider that best meets the needs of your organization, Wildlife Rescue International (WRI).

The Solution

In this project, you will learn how to get connected to the Internet and choose the Internet access provider that best meets the needs of your company, Wildlife Rescue International.

Evaluating Modems

Depending on when you bought your computer, it may or may not have come with a modem preinstalled inside it. Nowadays, any system you buy (except for laptop systems) almost unfailingly comes with an internal modem, some fax software, and one or two disks for online service providers that will connect you to the Internet.

If you bought a computer with an internal modem, you will most likely find the phone jack in the back of the computer. You can plug a phone cord into the phone jack in the modem unit and connect it with the phone line. If you bought an external modem, then you should connect it to the computer and phone line according to the instructions in the box.

 Reminder Modems are needed to convert digital computer signals into signals that can be transferred over analog phone lines. Many newer buildings have digital phone lines installed while the older buildings still have analog lines. If your phone line is digital, then you may not need a modem. Check with a systems administrator at your school for assistance and further information.

 Reminder You should also make sure that your modem's **_driver_** is correctly installed. A driver is special software on your computer that tells the computer how to communicate with the modem's hardware. Check your modem's documentation for directions.

Your modem unit communicates with your computer through a **_serial interface_**, or **_communications (COM) port_**, of the computer. COM ports are used to connect a number of different computer peripherals like a mouse or drawing tablet, so your computer will probably have more than one such port. If you have an internal modem, the modem is directly connected to a COM port inside the computer. If you have an external modem, then you must connect it to the COM port on the back of the computer. Figure 1.1 shows a picture of an external COM port. On the other end, the unit communicates with the phone line and, eventually, another modem located at your Internet access provider.

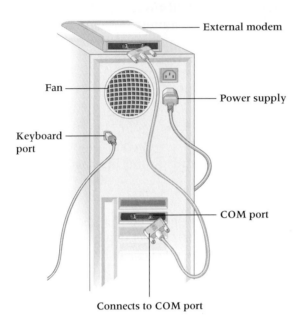

External modem

Fan

Power supply

Keyboard port

COM port

Connects to COM port

Figure 1.1

You should consider three main factors when buying a modem: (1) *transmission speed*, (2) *error control*, and (3) *data compression*. All three of these factors should follow the "V-dot" international standards established by the International Telecommunications Union's Study Group 14 (ITU SG14).

Transmission speed for modems is measured in bits per second (bps) or kilobits per second (kbps, 1 kbps = 1,024 bps). The newest modems optimally transfer files at 33.6 kbps or 28.8 kbps, but many people still access the Internet using 14.4 kbps or 9,600 bps modems. For your reference, the V-dot standards for transmission speed are shown in Table 1.1.

Table 1.1   V-dot Standard Equivalents for Transmission Speed

V-dot Standard	Transmission Speed
V.22bis	2,400 bps
V.32	9,600 bps
V.32bis	14.4 kbps
V.34	28.8 kbps
V.34 Enhanced	33.6 kbps

The standard that is currently being used for error control is *V.42*. The messages sent by your computer are broken up or divided into smaller units that may become corrupted. The V.42 standard establishes a method of detecting and correcting these errors during the transmission of messages over your modem.

The second generation of V.42 is called *V.42bis;* it is the standard used to compress transmitted data. The term *data compression* means that the modem sending the data recognizes common elements in the data and replaces the elements with shorter codes. The receiving modem then recognizes the codes and translates them back into the original elements. The transfer of these smaller files over the phone lines makes more efficient use of your time.

When a modem initially dials up another modem, it communicates with the other modem to determine what standards it is using so that the two can establish a dialog based on the same standards. Therefore, having a modem that supports the V-dot standards is important.

Credit card–sized *PC card* modems are also available if you have a laptop with PC card slots. Figure 1.2 shows such a modem. PC card standards are developed by the *Personal Computer Memory Card International Association (PCMCIA)* and cover all implementations of the PC card including memory expansion, storage expansion, and modem and fax use. Although these small modems may not have all the features that the bigger modems have, they are usually just as technically sound. The main problem with these small modems is that they may have hardware compatibility problems with certain laptops, so be sure to check with the laptop manufacturer for known problems before purchasing a PC card modem.

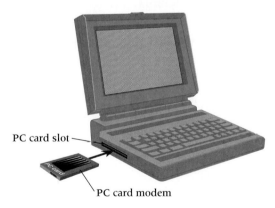

PC card slot

PC card modem

Figure 1.2

The following general rules may help alleviate problems when you're buying a modem:

- Buy a modem that is in full compliance with the V-dot standards.
- Be careful when buying a PC card for a laptop. Some compatibility issues are a concern, so check with the laptop manufacturer to obtain a list of compatible cards.

- Keep in mind that, if you're not very familiar with computer architecture, you should buy an external modem. It is easier to install and more convenient to use if you need to share it with another computer.
- If you can't afford to buy a 33.6 kbps modem, try to buy a modem that you can upgrade. Ask the vendor or salesperson whether the modem you're buying can be upgraded to 33.6 kbps. If you can't upgrade it, ask whether the manufacturer has trade-in options. Not many manufacturers offer trade-in options, but some do, so inquiring about such offers is worth your time.
- In Project 3, "Introduction to the World Wide Web," you will learn how the large file sizes of some Web pages and graphics can slow down your surfing. If you plan to access the WWW often, buying at least a 28.8 kbps modem is probably worth your investment.

TASK 1: TO EVALUATE THE PURCHASE OF A MODEM FOR WILDLIFE RESCUE INTERNATIONAL

1 Look through some computer magazines, and find some modem advertisements. Narrow your choices down to two modems. If you already have a modem, compare your modem with one advertised modem.

2 Research the two modems to make sure they conform to the V-dot standards and fall within your allocated budget. If you're looking at PC cards, be sure to contact your laptop's manufacturer regarding its compatibility with these modems.

3 Based on what you have learned in this section, and your evaluation of the advertised modems, choose one modem to purchase or to keep your own modem.

4 Open a word processing document, and start a new file.

5 At the top of the document, type **Connecting to a Service Provider**.

6 Enter this header: **Purchasing Modems**.

7 Under that header, type a summary describing the model and make of the modem that you have decided to purchase and why you decided to choose it. Or discuss why your current system is sufficient for Internet access without having to purchase a new modem.

8 Save this document with the file name SP.doc, and close your word processing program.

Understanding the Physical Setup of the Internet

In 1985, the National Science Foundation (NSF) decided to create a network that would link its five supercomputer centers for research purposes. This network came to be known as NSFNet, and its initial data transmission speed was a mere 56 kbps—just twice the speed of a 28.8 kbps modem.

As more educational and commercial institutions connected their own regional networks to NSFNet, the data transmission speed was upgraded to 1.544 Megabits per second (Mbps, 1 Mbps = 1,024 kbps). This high-speed line is commonly called a T1. Three years later, the transmission speed was increased to 45 Mbps, or T3. Two years after that, NSF stopped funding the project, and the Internet became largely funded by independent big businesses, universities, and the government.

Now the *Internet backbone* centers around *network access points (NAPs)* and other high-speed access points across the nation, as illustrated in Figure 1.3. A *backbone operator* must pay for and maintain high-speed lines that link to these access points. The more *redundancy*, or repeat connections, to these points, the more stable the network will be because the repeated connections can be used to reroute information if one connection goes down.

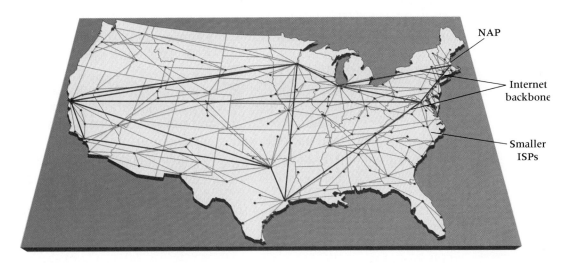

NAP

Internet backbone

Smaller ISPs

Figure 1.3

MCI, Sprint, UUNET, AGIS, ANS, and BBN are some of the national backbone operators. They lease their high-speed lines to online service providers or Internet service providers across the country. These providers then, in turn, can lease their connections to other smaller ISPs or directly to the public by means of Internet access accounts.

Learning About OSPs and ISPs

Online service providers (OSPs) and Internet service providers (ISPs) can both provide you with access to the Internet, but you will find some fundamental differences between the services they offer, and each has its own advantages and disadvantages. One disadvantage that is generally true for all providers, however, involves the struggle with the quality of their connectivity to the Internet due to the incredibly fast growth of the user base. This seemingly exponential growth has put an incredible load on the organizations' servers and **bandwidth**, and this load often translates into busy signals and slow access. Bandwidth is the amount of data that can be sent over the data lines and is usually an important limiting factor on Internet communications. Currently, most of these companies are scurrying to upgrade their hardware and software to keep up with the high demand and to remain competitive.

Online Service Providers

Online services such as America Online (AOL), Prodigy, CompuServe (also known as CSi, where the "i" stands for "interactive"), and Microsoft Network (MSN) provide services beyond Internet access. Currently, Internet access is just a small part of their services, but as the demand for access to the Internet increases, these online services are being forced to trade in their **proprietary**, or service-specific, look and content for the look and content that seamlessly blends with the Internet. Their extra services—including online sports information, stock market information, interactive games, and encyclopedic information—will have to be updated to follow the standards of the Internet.

Because all the options you face with the Internet can be overwhelming and confusing, you might want to get an Internet account with an online service provider if you prefer a well-organized tour of the Internet. OSPs' resources are set up for easy access to both their own services and Internet information.

A further advantage of OSPs is that, because of their large user bases, they have many dial-up phone numbers all over the country for travelers who don't want to make long distance calls but need to log into their accounts.

In their struggles to remain popular, AOL, Prodigy, and MSN have opted to offer their services for a low, unlimited use, monthly fee that competes with other, more inexpensive Internet service providers. Because CompuServe has decided to refocus its efforts on the business community, it is keeping its original per-hour pricing plan.

Of the four online service providers, CompuServe has always had its strongest relationship with the business community and was once the top contender in the battle of the online services. In an attempt to regain popularity, the company is going back to its previous clientele. However, in addition to its strong business content, CompuServe will also provide recreational content for business people to fill their non-working hours. Overall, CompuServe provides over 3,000 different services for its members.

AOL (America Online) has always focused more on the family and individual, and it will continue to do so. This service, shown in Figure 1.4, plans to gain more attention by increasing the interactive personality of its site. Additionally, because AOL wants the entire family to participate in the online experience, it is also supporting a more controlled environment in which parents can lock children out of certain areas of the network. AOL is very receptive to parent comments and questions.

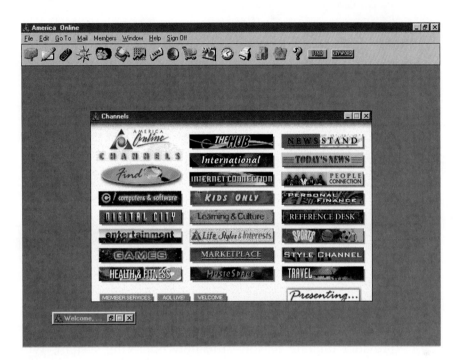

Figure 1.4

Prodigy, which was created by IBM and Sears, will continue to provide its regular family-based content, but it will also focus more of its energy on the international and cultural front. The company feels it will be gaining access not only to the international population, but also to a segment of the U.S. population that also wants international information. Figure 1.5 shows a Prodigy screen.

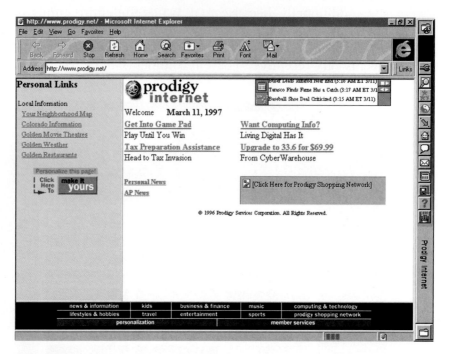

Figure 1.5

The Microsoft Network has gained a foothold in the online service industry through no real effort of its own. People have largely flocked to this provider for one reason—the new operating system, Windows 95, that came with their new computers prompted them to sign on. If you purchased a computer with Windows 95 preinstalled, then the MSN icon is already on your desktop waiting for you to double-click it to get online with the Microsoft Network. Microsoft also plans to extend MSN to the Macintosh and Windows NT operating systems. Unlike the other online service providers, MSN does not see its future as an Internet access provider. Rather, it will focus most of its energy on its own content and eventually shift Internet access responsibilities to another provider.

Online services sound too good to be true—organized access to the Internet and a myriad of other services for the same price as access to the Internet alone. They also provide local access to most places in the United States. Although the prices and the services can be very attractive, these services definitely have some drawbacks.

Online services present a lot of proprietary information that requires proprietary software, that is, special software used only by that particular online service. Although these services are trying to increase the flexibility of their software requirements, they can't completely discard the need for some rigidity and therefore will most likely always have rules for software use. Even those service providers that may allow people to use their own Internet software still require that you have their proprietary software installed to actually connect to the Internet and to view other non-Internet content. These proprietary software packages are often bulky and require a lot of hard disk space.

When you choose an online service, you are basically trading the flexibility of an average ISP for the organization of a large, multifaceted service. If you absolutely must have the newest program to run on the Internet, you probably belong with an Internet service provider that doesn't limit your options to its proprietary software.

Another additional drawback is that online services do not provide high-speed connections to the Internet. Generally, the highest speeds they service are 28.8 and 33.6 kbps. Therefore, an online service would not be a good choice for a business network that needs a faster, dedicated connection, for example.

If you have decided that the advantages of using an OSP outweigh the disadvantages, then you have taken one giant step toward getting connected. Choosing among the different online services can be tricky. Although we have outlined the main differences between the services, please be aware that the industry is constantly changing as the services try to gain a firmer foothold in the market. All of the services are constantly readjusting their approach toward content and their audience.

There was a recent attempt at a merger between AOL and CompuServe which ran into a snag and there have been rumors that CompuServe is taking another stab at providing content focused on the family.

Since it is pretty much impossible to make predictions about which way the tide will turn in this market, you should try to be an attentive consumer who keeps your eyes on the changing marketplace. Remember that your e-mail address will be based on one of these services and you don't want to have to contact all of your friends with the address change if your service goes under or gets bought out.

National and Regional ISPs

Several big businesses such as AT&T, IBM, Sprint, Earthlink, Netcom, and MCI are elbowing for a share of the Internet access market. They either currently provide or plan to soon provide both high-speed and low-speed access to the Internet as well as support for personal and business Web pages. Because these businesses are so big, their markets are nationwide or regionwide.

Like online services, Internet service providers often have many access numbers across the United States and even in other countries—a feature that can be very helpful to the frequent traveler. Additionally, subscribers also have access to toll-free access numbers for a small hourly fee. This service is especially useful for mobile businesses that need access to the Internet but do not want phone charges to appear on their clients' bills.

Although the initial setup package for ISPs may come with software for e-mail and Web browsing, unlike online services, their access accounts do not usually depend on proprietary software, so you have the flexibility (and responsibility) of buying and upgrading your own software. You can probably even dial up to the ISP using your operating system's dialing programs, as shown in Figure 1.6.

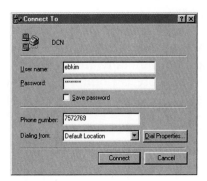

Figure 1.6

 Caution Although most ISPs do not require you to install proprietary software, some may insist that you use some of their software such as dial-up programs and e-mail programs. Therefore, asking an ISP (and even an OSP) about this issue before you sign on is always a good idea.

These national and regional providers are good choices for businesses and individuals who want flexible, high-speed access to the Internet.

Local ISPs and FreeNets

Many local ISPs have most of the services, including high-speed connections and Web presence options, that you find in a national or regional ISP, but they usually do not have local access numbers in more than two or three locations. The main draws of a local ISP are service and accessibility.

Some local ISPs across the country also provide varying levels of free access to the Internet. These ISPs are termed *FreeNets* and are usually centered around the community. They are often available as part of a local library or a community center, and have most likely been formed using volunteer time, community contributions, and free hardware contributions. Figure 1.7 shows the welcome screen for the Eugene FreeNet.

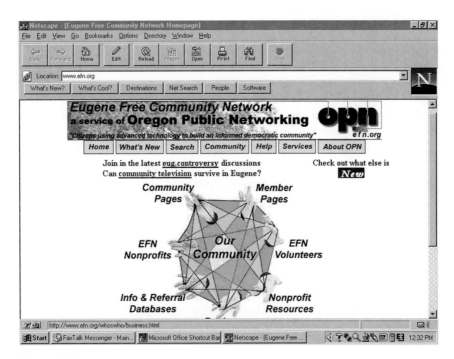

Figure 1.7

Tip In Project 4, "Searching the World Wide Web," you will learn searching techniques that will help you locate FreeNets and other Internet service providers. You can also use the skills you learn to research those organizations. Surfing the World Wide Web is a great substitute for using a phone—you can find almost all the information you need to know on the WWW and save the hard questions for a quick phone call.

Another great resource for researching and locating ISPs is the *Internet Access Providers Quarterly Directory* put out by *Boardwatch Magazine*. This directory lists service providers by area code and even answers many of the questions you may have. For example, you can find a provider's backbone operator and the speed of its connection. You can pick up this magazine at a local magazine stand.

Although FreeNets provide a wonderful community service (because people who can't pay for the services can still have access to the Internet), many FreeNets provide restricted access or even charge a small fee for some types of access. For example, because a FreeNet may be centered around a library without a modem pool for dial-up service, individual services such as e-mail may not be supported, but general Internet access is available. In other cases, a nonprofit corporation may have not only a dial-up modem pool, but also all the options of the Internet available to any community members.

FreeNets vary widely in their implementation of Internet access. Before you settle on any specific FreeNet or other ISP, go to a library that offers access to the WWW or to the house of a friend who has access to the Internet, and do a search for FreeNets in your area.

Schools

Almost all higher education institutions provide their students, staff, and faculty with free access to the Internet. Because educational institutions were among the first organizations to use the Internet, access through universities is generally good. All the options of the Internet usually are available through a fast, though often taxed, full-time connection while you're on campus or a modem while you're at home. The major drawback to this type of connection, however, is that it is usually terminated soon after you leave the institution.

The Internet on Your TV

Is the cost of a computer or the fear of operating one keeping you from surfing the Internet? Well, some companies have come up with options for you to go online using your television set.

Set-top systems, such as WebTV, allow you to access the Internet. These systems plug into your television and come with proprietary browser software and an optional keyboard that is necessary if you want to write e-mail messages. These systems often also require that you sign up with a particular ISP to use the system.

The available systems can range from anywhere between $200 and $1,000.

TASK 2: TO EVALUATE THE ACQUISITION OF AN INTERNET ACCESS PROVIDER FOR WILDLIFE RESCUE INTERNATIONAL

1 Open your word processing document and open the file SP.doc.

2 Add a new header called **Choosing an Internet Access Provider - Before Contact.**

3 Under this header, type a summary that describes what access provider you have chosen and why.

4 Enter this new header: **Choosing an Internet Access Provider - During Contact.**

5 Call up the access provider you have chosen and ask them the following questions.

 Caution Part of an evaluation of a service provider should include an evaluation of its customer service and technical support department. If the service provider can't answer the questions you're posing now, it probably will have trouble answering questions you may have later.

Question Set 1: How Fast and Consistent Is Your Connection?

1. How are you connected to the Internet backbone? What speed (T1 or T3)?

 Caution Speed isn't everything. Pay close attention to the other answers given to questions in this section. A T3 connection doesn't do you any good if the provider has saturated it with a large dial-up clientele.

2. How many modems do you have into which customers can dial?
3. How many customers do you have for dial-up access?
4. How often do your customers get a busy signal? (Get the dial-up modem pool phone number from the ISP, and call it at different times during the day to test how busy it is.)
5. How many Web sites do you host?

 Tip An ISP that hosts many World Wide Web pages may be slower than one that does not.

Question Set 2: How Is Your Customer Service?

1. What's your policy on people who send unwanted e-mail? Will you block them from your system after they are reported?
2. What's the average number of years of experience your technical support and network operations center staff have?
3. Do you have a 24-hour technical support line?
4. Do you have e-mail and Web technical support options?
5. Do you support options for parent-blocking programs?

Question Set 3: Miscellaneous Questions

1. Do you charge a flat rate, or do you charge by the hour?
2. Do you have a free trial period?
3. Do you have a setup fee?
4. What kind of software do you include in your offer?
5. Do you require use of proprietary software, or can users choose their own Web browser and e-mail client?
6. How long has your company been in business?

 Reminder Because your e-mail address will most likely be based on your access provider's name, you will want to keep that service for as long as you can. Like moving from state to state, if you do change service providers too often, keeping track of you becomes hard for your family and friends. Make sure you feel confident that the company will be around for as long as you are. Remember that this industry is young, and most of the smaller companies have existed for only about two years.

7. Do you have a local number in the area?
8. How many dial-up numbers do you have across the country and in other countries?
9. Do you provide an 800 number travelers can call for Internet access?
10. How much does access to the 800 number cost?

6 Make sure you fully investigate any responses that warrant further research. For example, after you ask for a dial-up phone number, call it at various times during the day to check whether you get a busy signal.

7 After you complete your investigation, add a new header called **Choosing an Internet Access Provider - After Contact** to your word processing document.

8 Summarize your impressions of the access provider, and discuss whether you would still consider using it and why.

9 Save your work, and close the word processing program.

Conclusion

Now that you've completed Project 1, review your work, read the summary, and do the following exercises.

Summary and Exercises

Summary

- Your modem communicates with your computer through the serial interface, or COM port, of the computer.
- Both 28.8 kbps and 33.6 kbps modems should conform to the V.34 standard for transmission speed.
- V.42 is the "V-dot" standard for error correction.
- V.42bis is the "V-dot" standard for data compression.
- Credit card-sized PC cards for laptops follow standards set forth by the Personal Computer Memory Card International Association (PCMCIA).
- The Internet backbone centers around Network Access Points (NAPs) that were designed by the National Science Foundation (NSF).
- The four major online service providers are CompuServe, America Online, Prodigy, and the Microsoft Network. OSPs offer Internet access as well as many other services.
- Some regional and local Internet service providers provide access only to the Internet. Many local ISPs allow access at little or no charge and, therefore, are termed FreeNets.
- Set-top systems allow you to access the Internet over a television set.

Key Terms

backbone operator	proprietary
bandwidth	redundancy
communications (COM) port	serial interface
data compression	set-top systems
driver	transmission speed
error control	V.22bis
FreeNet	V.32
Internet access provider	V.32bis
Internet backbone	V.34
network access point (NAP)	V.34 enhanced
online service provider	V.42
PC card	V.42bis
Personal Computer Memory Card	
International Association (PCMCIA)	

Study Questions

Multiple Choice

1. Which online service provider (OSP) caters most to the business community?
   a. America Online
   b. Prodigy
   c. Microsoft Network
   d. Davis Community Network
   e. CompuServe

2. V.42 is the standard for
   a. 28.8 kbps transmission speed.
   b. data compression.
   c. error correction.
   d. 33.6 kbps transmission speed.
   e. serial interfaces

3. Network access points (NAPs)
   a. were designed by Sprint.
   b. are connected only to university networks.
   c. are used for low-speed, low-cost phone connections to the Internet.
   d. are important points on the Internet backbone.
   e. all the above.

4. Internet service providers
   a. require users to use proprietary software.
   b. are solely dedicated to Internet access for researchers.
   c. cost more than online service providers.
   d. are generally the most flexible Internet access providers.
   e. all the above.

5. What speed modem is the fastest?
   a. 33.6 kbps
   b. 9,600 bps
   c. 28.8 kbps
   d. 2,400 bps
   e. 14.4 kpbs

6. To view the Internet over a television set, you need
   a. a FreeNet access provider
   b. a separate phone line
   c. a satellite dish
   d. a CD-ROM drive
   e. a set-top system

7. A backbone operator must:
   a. provide Internet access for $20 per month
   b. provide Internet access to businesses
   c. provide both Internet access and phone service
   d. fund high-speed lines connected to NAPs
   e. have 24-hour customer service

8. A good Internet service provider should
   a. have a high-speed connection to a backbone operator.
   b. have 24-hour technical support.
   c. allow parent-blocking programs.
   d. monitor for and reprimand junk e-mailers.
   e. all the above.

9. If choosing your own software is important to you, then you should access the Internet through
   a. America Online.
   b. a regional Internet service provider.
   c. a set-top system.

    d. the Microsoft Network.

    e. none of the above.

10. Redundancy

    a. causes breaks in Internet connectivity.

    b. causes a slowdown in transmission speed.

    c. helps stabilize the network.

    d. clears up noise coming over a modem.

    e. is required of online service providers.

Short Answer

1. Define ISP.

2. Outline how a modem works.

3. Define bps.

4. Name the V-dot standard for error correction.

5. What is the criterion to be a backbone operator?

6. What advantages do OSPs and national and regional ISPs have for travelers?

7. PCMCIA creates the standards for what system?

8. Name the four major OSPs.

9. Define set-top system.

10. A T3 line transfers data at what speed?

For Discussion

1. Discuss the advantages and disadvantages of using an online service such as AOL or CompuServe for your Internet access.

2. Discuss why you might choose a regional ISP for your Internet access.

3. Discuss the pros and cons of using a company such as AT&T for your Internet access.

4. What advantages do set-top systems have over regular computer systems?

5. Explain why the selection of your Internet access provider is an important decision.

Review Exercises

1. Investigating Online Services

Use magazine reviews, interview subscribers, or log on to one of the four large online services—Prodigy, CompuServe, America Online, and the Microsoft Network—to evaluate their ease of use, availability of help, services, customer support, and ease of canceling a subscription. You can go to their respective Web sites to download a free trial version of their software or use one of the many disks that come in computer magazines.

2. Examining FreeNets

In many communities, nonprofit corporations or libraries use FreeNets. Check for one in your area, and if you cannot find a FreeNet there, find the closest one. Gather information about the FreeNet, and write a paper using the research to tell how it works, who runs it, what it costs, and what is provided.

Assignments

1. Getting Connected

In this project, you learned about modems and phone connections. Use the information in this project to rate your personal modem if you have one or to find your ideal modem. Use speed, features, and compliance with standards for your rating. Write a brief description of your modem's rating.

2. Using a Personal Internet Account

In this project, you learned how to find the best ISP match for a business Internet account. Use the information that you learned in this project to find the best ISP match for your own personal Internet access account. Remember to look at on-line services (such as AOL and CompuServe), large companies with Internet access accounts (such as AT&T, IBM, and MCI), and regional services (such as your town's local nonprofit Internet access organization). After looking at the available service providers in your area, write an evaluation of your top two choices.

What Does It Cost?

Excerpt from an article by Robin Frost. Reprinted by permission of The Wall Street Journal, *December 9, 1996, copyright 1996 Dow Jones & Company, Inc. All rights reserved worldwide.*

How much does it cost to go on-line?

If you're just getting started in cyberspace and already have a PC, it seems like an easy question: a hundred dollars or so for a modem, maybe $20 a month for a service provider, and that's that.

But the price question is actually more complicated. There are hardware decisions to make long before you get a modem that will affect your bill considerably. Service providers vary widely in the prices—and options—they offer. After you have chosen a service, there are still more charges that can crop up.

So, to help you along, here's a look at exactly how much it will cost you to catch the wave in cyberspace.

To begin with, there's the seemingly obvious question of what kind of computer you need. The question to ask yourself: Just how detailed do you want your cruises through cyberspace to be?

The old 486 machine lurking on the desktop is fine if all you're interested in is reading newsgroups on the Internet or traveling to text-heavy World Wide Web sites; even a creaky 386 is fine for downloading e-mail. But if you want to experience all the bells and whistles on the Web—file and music clips, 3-D sites, animation—you're going to have to make big investments in new hardware.

The key word to buying a computer for high-level surfing: multimedia. You'll need a good graphics card and sound card—pieces of hardware that let your computer show pictures or play sounds—stereo speakers, a huge hard drive (one or two gigabytes), 32 megabytes of memory and at least a four-speed CD-ROM drive. (Why the CD-ROM? Some disks let you update their software by accessing a Web site.) For PC users, it is advisable to go with Microsoft Corp.'s Windows '95 operating system; many Web software applications require it. This package should set you back $2,000 to $3,000.

Another key word is speed. Your machine's processor chip should be fast—at least 120 megahertz, and faster won't hurt given the rapid evolution of Internet applications. A 14.4-kilobit-per-second modem, usually the basic speed, costs under $100, and is fine for rifling newsgroups or even browsing, if you don't mind waiting a couple of minutes for graphics-heavy pages to download. If you want to keep the Web animation fairly brisk and downloads as short as possible, get the current standard for most companies—a 28.8 modem. It will cost under $200. For the fastest standard modems, some companies are offering 33.6-kbps models for $200 to $300.

E-mail

In this project, you will learn the history of electronic mail (e-mail), how it works, and the important features of e-mail software. You will also learn the purpose of mailing lists.

Objectives

After completing this project, you will be able to do the following:

➤ **Discuss the history of e-mail and how it works**

➤ **Discuss how free e-mail service providers handle e-mail**

➤ **Discuss the purpose of mailing lists**

The Challenge

When you hear about the Internet these days, you most likely hear people talking about the World Wide Web (discussed in Project 3, "Introduction to the World Wide Web" and Project 4, "Searching the World Wide Web"). However, despite the Web's glitz and glamour, fewer people use it than use e-mail. In only a few years, e-mail has become a critical part of business and personal communication—in many cases, it is even more important than telephone communication.

E-mail is convenient for sending memos, scheduling meetings, and just keeping in touch. One of the nicest features of e-mail is that you can send detailed information that the receiver can prioritize and then process in a timely manner. You don't have to talk to the person, leave lengthy messages on voice mail that the recipient then must write down, or wait for a return phone call. After the person receives the message, completes a project, or whatever she has to do, she can just e-mail you back a response.

As part of your investigation of the Internet for Wildlife Rescue International, you must research e-mail, learn to use it, and present a summary to the director.

The Solution

In this project, you will learn about e-mail. Periodically during your research, you will e-mail the director a written summary of your progress.

Exploring E-mail

The format of an e-mail address is generally *name@domain.xxx*, where *xxx* is the three-letter abbreviation for an organization type such as edu, com, or net. (For a review of domains, see the Overview.) Computers essentially read the e-mail address **jsmith@ucla.edu** from right to left. First, they see that the message is directed toward an educational institution. Then they see that the educational institution is UCLA. Last, they find jsmith's e-mail account at UCLA and deliver the message.

E-mail is sent over the Internet using **Simple Mail Transfer Protocol (SMTP)**, which was standardized in 1983. SMTP completely conforms to the rules set by TCP/IP, which governs the transfer of data over the Internet. SMTP's sole purpose is to get the e-mail message from the sender's machine to the receiver's mail server. When a message is sent out, it is broken up into packets according to TCP/IP standards. These packets are sent through varying paths and eventually end up at the receiver's mail server where they are reassembled into the original information. However, these packets may arrive at different times because the path that one packet takes may have slow points, whereas the path another packet takes may be ideal. Because of these variable arrival times and the fact that some packets may not make it at all and must be requested again by the receiving computer, delivery time is not guaranteed. Additionally, SMTP will not allow you to read your attachments, allow you to delete a message that you've already sent, or send you a return message stating that the e-mail was successfully received. (All of these features will be discussed later in this project.)

After a message reaches the mail server, SMTP's job is done. Getting the mail from the server to the receiver's machine is the job of two other protocols: **Post Office Protocol (POP)** and **Internet Message Access Protocol (IMAP)**. The most recent versions of these protocols are POP3 and IMAP4.

Think of the mail account on your server as a P.O. box. The mail carrier doesn't bring the mail in that box to your house. You have to go to the post office to check the box for mail. Although you still have to take the initiative to check the mailbox, you can send POP or IMAP to the post office to get the mail for you.

The major difference between POP and IMAP is that IMAP is more advanced. Instead of just taking all the mail off the server as POP does, IMAP allows you to read through messages and choose which messages you want to *download*, or transfer to your computer from the mail server, and which messages you want to leave on the server. Furthermore, it even allows you to download selected parts of messages rather than entire messages. These options are helpful if you're sharing a mail account with several people and want to share information. However, IMAP is not widely implemented yet. Although most Internet service providers plan to support IMAP in the future, for now, most support only POP.

Although e-mail communication may replace telephone communication in many circumstances, you can't depend on it if the information you need is time-critical, because you get no guarantees on delivery time. You might send out a message that calls for a mandatory emergency meeting in 8 hours, but the message may not reach the recipient's mail account for 24 hours or may even bounce back to you if delivery errors occurred. Furthermore, unless you can require that a person read e-mail every few hours, you also have no guarantee that the recipient will check messages in time to make the meeting. When a prompt response is necessary, just using a pager or phone may be better until Internet standards that can guarantee timely delivery of information are developed.

TASK 1: TO UPDATE THE WRI DIRECTOR ON YOUR PROGRESS

1 Open a word processing program, and create a new document.

2 At the top of the document, enter the date.

3 As in a memo, address the TO: field to the director.

4 Under the TO: field, type **FROM:** and your name.

5 Under the FROM: field, type **RE: A History of E-mail and Its Protocols**. RE is short for "regarding" and states the subject of the message.

6 In your own words, write a short paragraph describing each of the following items: the anatomy of e-mail; SMTP; POP and IMAP.

7 Sign the memo with your name.

8 Save the file as MEMO.doc, and close the word processing program.

Common Software Features

E-mail programs have come a long way from the days of menu-driven simple text programs like Pine (see Figure 2.1). These days, e-mail programs can do anything from presenting a simple e-mail message to

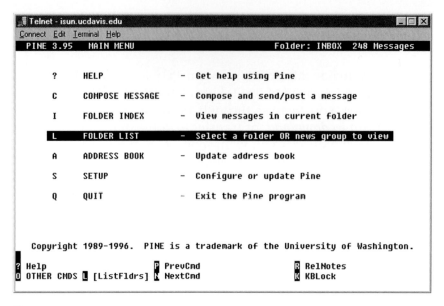

Figure 2.1

launching a Web browser, scanning attachments for viruses, encrypting e-mail messages, and faxing documents. In the following sections, you'll learn about common features that are now available in many e-mail programs. Although the e-mail program Eudora is used in the figures, many of these features are available in other programs as well.

Composing, Sending, and Receiving E-mail

This section will review the basics of using e-mail. Most of these features should be present in even the simplest e-mail programs.

SMTP/POP/IMAP Support

Proprietary e-mail programs—that is, programs that follow standards developed by the individual online service providers such as CompuServe—do not always use SMTP, POP, or IMAP. These online service providers usually developed their programs based on their own unique standards, and if they now include the Internet standards, they added them as an afterthought. Therefore, you have to use their software if you want to log on to their services.

If you use an Internet service provider such as a FreeNet, you can use any software package that supports SMTP or POP. Not all ISPs currently support the IMAP standard, although they will eventually.

DATE:, TO:, SENDER:, FROM:, REPLY-TO:, SUBJECT:, CC:, BCC:

The DATE:, TO:, SENDER:, FROM:, REPLY-TO:, SUBJECT:, CC:, BCC: entry fields are commonly found in the **header** of an e-mail message. E-mail messages are divided into two parts—header and **body**. As its name implies, the header comes at the beginning of the e-mail message and announces information such as whom the message is to, whom the message is from, and what the subject of the message is. The body contains the main text of the message.

If you are the person sending the message, your e-mail program automatically inserts the date and time that you send the message in the *DATE:* field. If you are the person receiving the message, you see the date and time stamp in the header of the message.

If you are sending the message, you should type in the receiver's e-mail address in the *TO:* field. If you want to send the message to more than one person, you can add e-mail addresses by placing commas between them.

 Tip Always check the TO: line to be sure that you have not inadvertently included anyone who should not receive the e-mail.

Surprisingly, the name that you see in the *SENDER:* field is not always the same as the name you see in the *FROM:* field or the *REPLY-TO:* field of a message you have received. For example, if you subscribe to a *mailing list* that distributes the message to a large group of people via e-mail, the names in these fields can vary. If you send a message to the mailing list, the list forwards the message to the entire discussion group. So, the e-mail address in the FROM: field is yours, but the address in the SENDER: field is the mailing list's because it actually performed the final send to the list members. Furthermore, depending on how the mailing list's software is configured, the REPLY-TO: field might contain your e-mail address so that people can automatically reply to you personally, or the mailing list's address so that the discussion can remain on the list.

The information that goes into the *SUBJECT:* field is extremely important. It can be the deciding factor for whether someone takes the time to read the message, so take care when you compose it. The information should be concise and informative, and it should convey urgency if the message is important. For example, don't just write "Hello, how're you feeling?" if you're sending information about a change in mandatory meeting dates to a co-worker who has been sick and hasn't been at work for a week. Instead, write "IMPORTANT: Mandatory Meeting Date Changed." This issue may seem trivial, but subject lines are very important to people who receive a lot of e-mail.

CC: is short for Carbon Copy. This field is used to send e-mail to people who should be made aware of the information in the e-mail message but to whom the e-mail is not directly addressed. The CC: field works just as it does in a paper memo; however, the message is sent automatically. Both the recipient named in the TO: field and the people who have been CC'd will be aware of the fact that the e-mail was sent to all parties.

When the Blind Carbon Copy (*BCC:*) field is used, however, the person named in the TO: field will not know that the e-mail was sent to other people. Figure 2.2 shows a message sent to a mailing list. Pay close attention to the header SENDER: and FROM: fields.

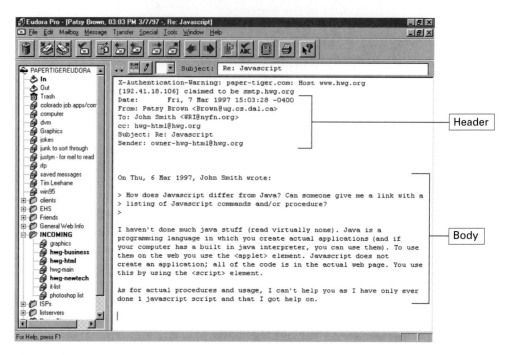

Figure 2.2

Reply, Reply All, Forward, Redirect

While viewing e-mail you have received, if you click on the **Reply** button, the original sender's e-mail address is moved to the TO: field, and your address is placed in the FROM: field.

If you click on the **Reply All** button, the original sender's e-mail address along with the addresses of anyone in the CC: field are placed in the TO: field, and your address is placed in the FROM: field.

Because both of these actions are performed automatically by the program, you should double-check the TO: field to ensure that the reply is actually going to the right person. Also, some e-mail programs automatically place the original text in the body of the reply message for reference purposes.

Using the **Forward** function, you have to place the person's e-mail address in the TO: field, but your e-mail address usually is automatically placed in the FROM: field. The body of the message always includes the original text, but you can excerpt information, modify, or add to the message.

The **Redirect** feature is handy, although it isn't included in every e-mail program. It's most useful in a scenario like the following. Say you're at work, and you receive an e-mail message that really should have been directed to a co-worker. When you click the Redirect button and put your co-worker's address in the TO: field, notice that the FROM: field now states something similar to "FROM: person@company.com by way of me@mycompany.com" (see Figure 2.3). In this way, you emphasize that the message really came from another person but that you read it and felt that it more appropriately belonged to someone else. You should not modify the message because it does not really belong to you. It is appropriate, however, for you to add a note at the beginning of the message explaining the circumstances to the receiver.

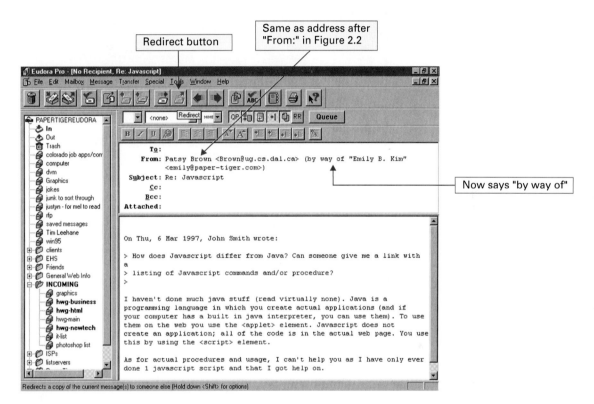

Figure 2.3

Attachments

Because SMTP can transfer only plain-text messages, how do you send more complex information such as word processing documents that include formatting and tables?

MIME (Multipurpose Internet Mail Extension), **BinHex**, and **UUENCODE** are all methods of **encoding** that translate these more complex documents into simple symbols that can be transferred using SMTP. These simplified files are then attached to the main e-mail message and so are called **attachments**.

All the encoding and **decoding** is done by the mail programs, not by the mail protocol, so you must have a program that supports one, or preferably all, of these encoding methods if you want to send non-text-based files. MIME is the newest method of encoding and the most common. BinHex is used mostly by Macintosh systems, and UUENCODE is used mostly by UNIX systems. A file must be decoded using the same method with which it was encoded, but using MIME as the encoding method is preferable.

Note that the **ATTACHED:** field in the header of the mail message in Figure 2.4 lists a file called Animals.tif in the WRI folder. Also note that the body of the message lets the recipient know that the file has been MIME-encoded.

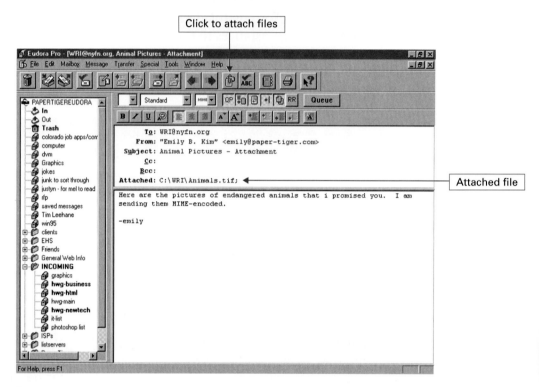

Figure 2.4

Spelling Checkers

You can probably find a spelling checker in almost all e-mail programs that you encounter. These spelling checkers are similar to the ones found in word processing programs. You can either run them manually after you compose the message, or you can have them automatically check every message before you send it. Checking every message before you send it to other people is a good idea.

 Tip Never put on (CAPS LOCK) to compose a message. Using all caps is considered shouting in cyberspace.

Priority Settings

Although a properly composed subject header should convey the urgency of a mail message, many e-mail programs also include **priority settings** that allow the sender to emphasize how important the message is. Not only do the settings allow you to state that a message is high priority, but they also let you state that the message is a low priority and can be read when the recipient has free time. Figure 2.5 shows a message that is marked at "Highest" priority.

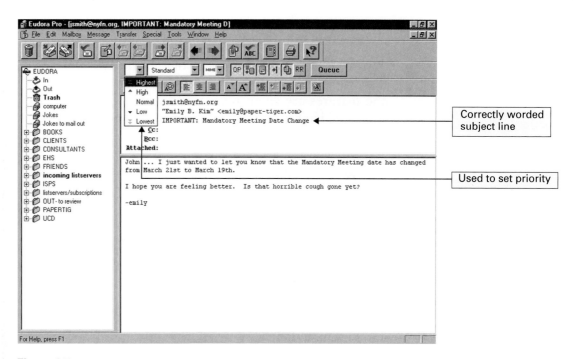

Figure 2.5

Signatures

Signatures are optional features that are typically placed at the end of the e-mail message and usually include contact information. Some people use them more casually by putting pictures or quotes in them. Usually, e-mail programs let you choose between two different signatures when you send out messages. Figure 2.6 shows two signatures—one with contact information and one with a more casual theme.

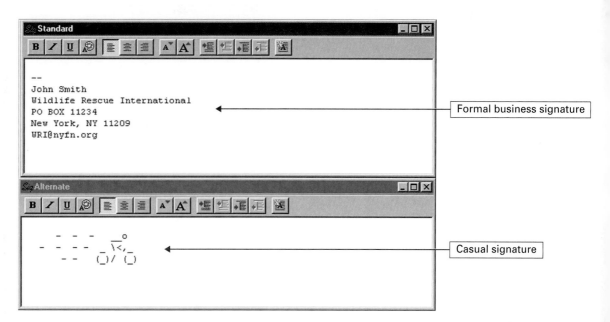

Figure 2.6

Managing E-mail

This section will review some of the more advanced features in e-mail programs that help you organize your messages. General explanations of the features are given here, and features in several e-mail programs are reviewed later in this project.

Filters

Filters are a handy feature for people who get a lot of e-mail messages. Most filters use the information in the headers of e-mail messages to sort through mail.

For example, you may receive a lot of e-mail jokes from your friend Patsy who works for IBM. Because you don't always have time to read these messages immediately, you can have all messages with the e-mail address **patsy@ibm.com** in the FROM: section of the header put into a different folder that you can read through later, as shown in Figure 2.7. This way, you can free up space in the e-mail ***inbox*** for messages that require immediate attention. The inbox is where messages first enter your program. They wait there to be read or processed by features like filters.

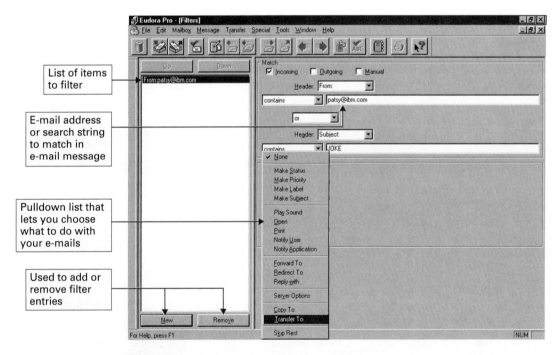

Figure 2.7

With more advanced software, you can sort through messages by filtering information that's not only in the headers of the e-mail messages, but also in the body of the messages.

Tip Always keep the e-mail inbox cleared out by deleting unwanted messages. To do so, you place them in the Trash folder. Most e-mail programs automatically flush the Trash folder, so don't place anything in the Trash folder that you might want in the future.

Nicknames

E-mail messages are often returned to the sender with an error message stating that the e-mail address the sender specified does not exist. On further inspection, you may note that a word was misspelled or an extra period or hyphen was added to the address. These types of errors are not only frustrating and annoying, but also waste precious time because you have to resend them and wait for the response.

With these points in mind, some software companies have implemented the *nicknames* option in their e-mail programs. The basic idea is that you associate an e-mail address with a nickname. For example, instead of having to type in **patsy@ibm.com** in the TO: field every time you want to send Patsy a message, you just type in the nickname that you have chosen for her. Because each program is different, it either automatically prompts you to add the e-mail address to the nicknames folder or allows you to add the information manually.

You also can use nested nickname files or *group names*. Say you usually announce information on endangered species, such as tigers, to all locations of WRI that need the information. You can save time by creating a group called Tiger and adding each e-mail address you want to the group. Then you can easily and quickly address the e-mail to the Tiger group.

Address Books

Group names are often combined with *address books* that allow you to address e-mail by selecting individuals or groups from the address book. Many e-mail software packages automatically add the e-mail address of anyone who sends you mail to the online address book. Also, you can easily create groups, such as the Tiger group, by simply clicking the names of people you want to include.

Figure 2.8 shows an address book that lists its contents by nicknames. From a program's address book window, you can start a new e-mail message and put this person's name in the TO:, CC:, or BCC: fields.

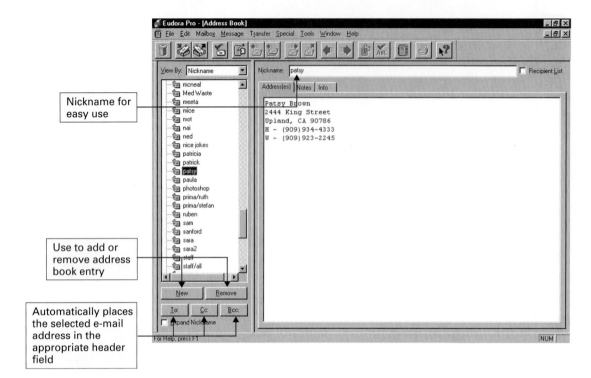

Nickname for easy use

Use to add or remove address book entry

Automatically places the selected e-mail address in the appropriate header field

Figure 2.8

Folder System

Folder systems in e-mail programs help you organize all the messages you receive into logical topics. Many programs allow you to have only one level of folders. Other programs allow you to build a ***nested folder system*** in which you can create a hierarchy of folders or subfolders. For example, if you're working on several projects, you might want to have a folder for correspondence that relates to each project. Because the volume of e-mail for any project could be quite large, you can then create subfolders for each project. The left side of Figure 2.9 shows a folder system. Note that the folders open into mailboxes that are essentially subfolders to the main topic.

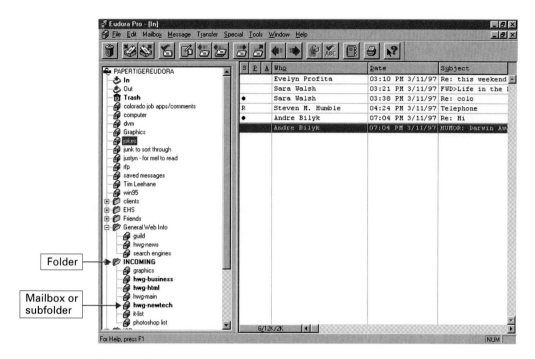

Figure 2.9

Extra Features

This section introduces more advanced features that you may find in your e-mail program. Although most of the e-mail programs we reviewed include these features, they are harder to find than the basic features discussed earlier.

Multiple E-mail Accounts

Having an e-mail program that can accept mail for multiple e-mail accounts is advantageous for families and small businesses or businesses in which employees share the same computer, because each person can have a private e-mail address, using the same account. Although this setup may mean buying a separate Internet access account for each individual who wants mail, check with your service provider because, although it may not widely advertise this capability, it may allow you to have multiple e-mail accounts as part of one Internet access account, thereby allowing each user to have his or her own e-mail address.

Some e-mail programs are designed for the purpose of maintaining multiple e-mail accounts including separate nicknames files, address books, and folder systems for each person.

Program Launch

As you begin to browse through the World Wide Web (discussed in Projects 3 and 4) and find files through File Transfer Protocol (FTP, discussed in Project 6*) you'll find the ability to launch other programs from within the mail program very useful. For example, when you receive an e-mail message that cites a Web address, that address appears as highlighted hypertext. When you click on the underlined Web address, you **launch** your default Web browser, and the page that the address points to is automatically loaded for your viewing pleasure, as shown in Figure 2.10.

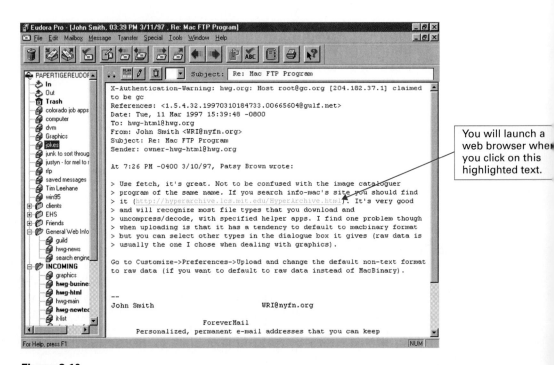

Figure 2.10

Program launches, however, are not only useful for surfing the Internet. When you receive attachments along with mail messages, a graphic icon or highlighted text notifies you that you have received an attachment with your message. You can then click on the notification, and the associated program is launched so that you can view the document.

Encryption

Encrypting e-mail messages helps you control who can and cannot read your mail.

Encryption is the means by which you scramble an e-mail message. The scrambling of messages is usually performed by complex mathematical processes. The message can only be unscrambled by the use of a **pass-**

---

*The *SELECT Lab Series: Projects for the Internet* is available in three versions: the Brief, which contains the Overview through Project 4, the regular, which contains the Overview through Project 8, and the Plus, which contains the Overview through Project 12. References to Projects 5–12 are asterisked in these pages to remind you that you can find them in the SELECT regular or SELECT Plus editions.

phrase, which is similar to a password except that it consists of an entire phrase, a password, or by the use of coded keys.

The method that uses computer-coded keys requires that you send a digital *public key* to anyone with whom you correspond. When that person sends you an e-mail message, he or she attaches your public key to it. You use your secret digital *private key* to verify the public key and to unlock the messages. Your private key is the only electronic code that will match the public key and unlock your messages.

Caution Many people think that sending e-mail is completely private because no paper is involved. However, remember that everything that has been sent over the Internet could exist in an archive somewhere. Never send anything using e-mail that you might not want made public later.

Virus Checker

Although your computer cannot be infected with a virus through use of regular text-based e-mail, it can be infected if you open or activate attachments that contain viruses.

Very few e-mail programs include built-in virus checkers. Therefore, you should install a separate virus checker on your computer system. These checkers can be configured to monitor your system constantly to detect any potentially harmful activity.

Fax Support

Although many e-mail programs support fax options, this does not mean that you are faxing over the Internet. Rather, a separate fax module in the program allows you to dial up a fax machine to transfer the file. You still accrue long distance charges regardless of whether you use the fax module inside the e-mail program or a stand-alone fax program.

TASK 2: TO WRITE A SIMPLE E-MAIL MESSAGE TO THE DIRECTOR OF WRI AND UPDATE HER ON WHAT YOU HAVE LEARNED

1 Open an e-mail program, and prepare to compose a new e-mail message.

2 In the TO: field of the e-mail program, type the e-mail address of the director of WRI.

3 In the Subject: field, type **Four Common E-mail Features**.

4 In the body of the text, summarize four of the e-mail features discussed in the preceding section using your own words.

5 Send the e-mail message, and close the e-mail program.

Free E-mail Services

Some new companies give you free e-mail accounts. They can afford to give out these accounts because advertisers pay for their operation expenses. You can compare this idea with television. It doesn't cost you more than the price of a television set to watch TV, because advertisers pay for commercials that essentially cover your costs.

With Juno, you use proprietary software to log on to the system and retrieve e-mail. The installation and interface, shown in Figure 2.11, are easy to use, even for beginners who have never before used their modems. You can download the program at Juno's Web site (http://www.juno.com) if you have access to the Internet.

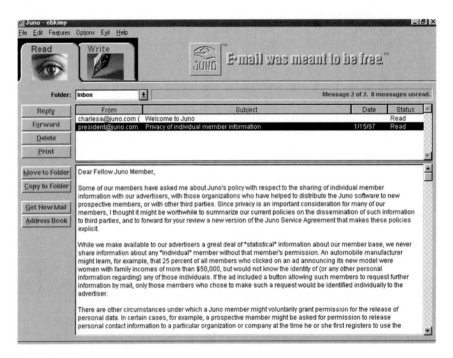

Figure 2.11

HoTMaiL, shown in Figure 2.12, and NetAddress also offer free e-mail services because they too use advertising money. However, their approach actually targets a different market. Neither of these systems uses proprietary e-mail software to access messages. They don't use SMTP-, POP-, or IMAP-compliant e-mail programs either. They actually use World Wide Web browsers (discussed in Project 3) as their e-mail interfaces.

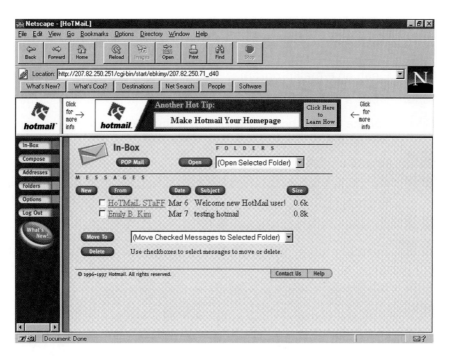

Figure 2.12

Yes, you need access to the Internet to use these free e-mail systems. You may think it is a little strange that they offer free e-mail because an e-mail account usually comes with your Internet access account. Both companies, however, are looking toward a time when free access to the Internet will be available from just about anywhere. When this time comes, you will be able to walk up to your local bank's ATM, do your banking, and check your e-mail at the same time. Many coffee shops and libraries already offer free access to the Internet, so you could easily check your e-mail over a donut and a cup of coffee.

NetAddress is also advertising a lifetime e-mail address. No matter which provider you use as an ISP, you can always use NetAddress to check your e-mail, so that address never has to change. Think of your e-mail address in the same way that you think about your house address. Keeping track of your home address is difficult for others if you keep moving. The same is true about your e-mail address. Keeping the same e-mail address for as long as you can is best.

Some people think that these systems (including Juno) are wonderful because they are free. Two major drawbacks, however, are that they are often slow and only HoTMail lets you send attachments—and then only if you use Netscape Navigator. Because they're free, you can try them out at your leisure and decide for yourself whether you like their interfaces and features.

You can sign on to HoTMaiL by accessing their Web site at http://www. hotmail.com. You can find NetAddress at http://www.netaddress.com.

TASK 3: TO EVALUATE SMTP, POP, AND IMAP E-MAIL PROGRAMS FOR WRI

1 Open an e-mail program.

2 Open a word processing program, and create a new document.

3 For the title of the document, enter the name of the e-mail program you're evaluating.

4 Create a table with two columns.

5 Name the first column **Features,** and then list all the features mentioned in the project.

6 Name the second column **Yes/No**.

7 Search through all the menus, toolbars, and help information to find out whether the program has the features mentioned.

8 Put a **Y** or **N** in the second column accordingly.

9 Print out your evaluation, and submit it to the director.

10 Close the e-mail program.

11 Save the document as POP.doc, and close the word processing program.

TASK 4: TO EVALUATE FREE E-MAIL BROWSER SERVICES FOR WRI

1 Open a Web browser.

2 Using the Web addresses given in the preceding section, visit the HoTMaiL or NetAddress Web site to sign up for one of the services.

3 Familiarize yourself with this Web-based e-mail program.

4 Evaluate the browser e-mail program for all the features mentioned in the preceding sections.

5 Open a word processing program, and open a new document.

6 For the title of the document, enter the name of the browser e-mail program you're evaluating.

7 Create a table with two columns.

8 Name the first column **Features,** and then list all the features mentioned in the project.

9 Name the second column **Yes/No**.

10 Search through all the menus, toolbars, and help information to find out whether the program has the features mentioned.

11 Put a **Y** or **N** in the second column accordingly.

12 Print out your evaluation, and submit it to the director.

13 Close the e-mail program.

14 Save the document as BROWSER.doc, and close the word processing program.

Mailing Lists, Listservers, and Listprocessors

As you've learned throughout this project, using e-mail is a great way to communicate with clients, co-workers, and friends. However, it is also useful for communicating with people on a much larger scale if you use mailing lists (which you read about briefly earlier in the project). Mailing lists are like discussion groups you might find on one of the newsgroups (discussed in Project 5*). With mailing lists, though, instead of your having to log on to the newsgroups, the messages people send come directly into your e-mail inbox.

If you're interested in joining a mailing list about bird watching (specifically the endangered species the spotted owl), for example, you can search the Web for information (searching the Web is discussed in Project 4). You then can subscribe to the mailing list by sending e-mail to the *listserver* or *listprocessor*. These software programs coordinate mailing lists. They keep a list of all the people who have subscribed to a particular mailing list and their e-mail addresses, and they forward messages to all of these people when someone sends e-mail to the list.

Say you found through your search on the Web that you must send a message to listserv@birdwatching.com to sign on to the list about owls. In the body of the message, you usually write something like this:

subscribe owls *yourfirstname yourlastname*

subscribe tells the listserver that you want to subscribe to the list called owls. You don't need to put any information into the subject line.

After you receive the confirmation of your subscription, you can then join the mailing list. Usually, you should *lurk* for a while; that is, read the messages from others and not send any mail until you feel confident that you understand the purpose of the mailing list and the mood of its subscribers. Once you feel comfortable, you can send a message to owls@birdwatching.com, and it will be distributed to everyone on the list. The other subscribers can then respond to you personally or to the entire list.

Although mailing lists are often most visibly used on large-scale projects in which you encounter people you don't know but who have similar interests, they are just as useful for small-scale communication with co-workers and colleagues. You can use mailing lists to distribute information and communicate with your department, a task force, or even a class if you're a teacher.

Conclusion

Now that you've completed Project 2, review your work, read the summary, and do the following exercises.

Summary and Exercises

Summary

- SMTP (Simple Mail Transfer Protocol) is the Internet protocol the determines how e-mail is sent.
- POP (Post Office Protocol) and IMAP (Internet Message Access Protocol) are the Internet protocols that determine how e-mail is downloaded from the server to your computer.
- A mail message consists of a header and a body.
- MIME (Multipurpose Internet Mail Extension), BinHex, and UUENCODE are the three most common methods for encoding attachments.
- Filters supply you with an automated way to sort through mail messages.
- Address books help you keep track of your e-mail correspondents.
- A nested folder system allows you to better organize e-mail messages.
- Encryption helps ensure that only you can read your e-mail.
- If your e-mail program does not support a virus checker, you should install one to check attachments for viruses.
- You can use signature files to attach contact information to the end of your e-mail messages.
- Juno, HoTMaiL, and NetAddress are three new companies that provide free e-mail. Juno has a proprietary e-mail program, but the other two are Web browser-based.
- Mailing lists allow you to communicate with several people at one time.

Key Terms

address book
ATTACHED:
attachments
BCC:
BinHex
body
CC:
DATE:
decoding
download
encoding
encryption
filters
Forward
FROM:
group names
header
inbox
Internet Message Access
    Protocol (IMAP)

launch
listprocessor
listserver
lurk
mailing list
MIME
nested folder system
nicknames
passphrase
Post Office Protocol (POP)
private key
public key
Redirect
Reply
REPLY-TO:
SENDER:
Simple Mail Transfer Protocol (SMTP)
SUBJECT:
TO:
UUENCODE

Study Questions

Multiple Choice

1. MIME is
   a. a protocol for mail transfer.
   b. an encryption mechanism.
   c. a virus checking program.
   d. a method of encoding attachments.
   e. the group that standardizes protocols.

2. A mailing list
   a. allows you to communicate with a maximum of only 10 people.
   b. uses the FTP protocol to transfer information.
   c. is browser-based.
   d. uses listservers or listprocessors to process messages.
   e. must use a WWW server to process messages.

3. What allows you to organize and maintain your correspondents' nicknames and personal information?
   a. filters
   b. address books
   c. mailing lists
   d. alphanumeric pagers
   e. headers

4. This is a document that is specially encoded for transfer over the Internet.
   a. attachment.
   b. passphrase.
   c. header.
   d. filter.
   e. address book.

5. What process often requires keys to unlock e-mail messages?
   a. scanning
   b. encoding
   c. processing
   d. encrypting
   e. transferring

6. What protocol allows you to sort through your e-mail messages before you download them and choose to leave some of them on the server?
   a. IMAP
   b. MIME
   c. SMTP
   d. POP
   e. TCP/IP

7. What is the underlying protocol on which the mail protocols are built?
   a. MIME
   b. SMTP
   c. POP
   d. TCP/IP
   e. IMAP

8. Viruses can infect your system if they are sent
   a. with plain e-mail messages
   b. with groups
   c. with encryption
   d. with attachments
   e. with filters

9. The header of an e-mail message always includes
   a. a subject.
   b. a body.
   c. a signature.
   d. a filter.
   e. an attachment.

10. Two common methods to encode attachment files are
    a. MIME and BinHex.
    b. UUENCODE and SMTP.
    c. TCP/IP and IMAP.
    d. BinHex and POP.
    e. IMAP and POP.

Short Answer

1. Discuss the different parts of the e-mail address anatomy: **aaaaaa@bbbbbbb.xxx**

2. How do free e-mail services pay for their expenses?

3. Explain what an application launch does.

4. Explain nested folders.

5. What keys are used in encryption?

6. What items commonly go in the header of an e-mail message?

7. When would you use the "Redirect" option?

8. Explain the difference between the POP and IMAP protocols.

9. What information would you send in the body of an e-mail message when subscribing to a mailing list?

10. How are address books helpful?

For Discussion

1. How are filters useful if you subscribe to many mailing lists?

2. How do e-mail programs deal with security issues?

3. Why are browser-based e-mail programs considered useful for the future?

4. Can viruses infect your system if you use e-mail?

5. Why should you check to see who is in the TO: line of all your mail?

Review Exercises

1. Composing, Proofreading, and Sending an E-mail Message

Open your e-mail program, and address an e-mail message to the director of Wildlife Rescue International. Be sure to include a Subject line. Compose a message and use any editing functions to correct errors. If possible, spell-check the message, and then send it to the director.

2. Subscribing to a Mailing List and Printing a Message

Wildlife Rescue International wants to have employees subscribe to existing mailing lists. Find a mailing list about endangered species or about a specific environmental issue affecting endangered species and subscribe to it. After you receive a message of interest from the list, print it out.

Assignments

1. Creating Groups and Sending E-mail to a Group

Use the address book in your e-mail program to create a group called *Students*. Place several students enrolled in your course in the group. Compose and send an e-mail to the group.

2. Replying and Forwarding E-mail Messages

After you receive a message from another student enrolled in the course, forward that message to another student.

Reply to the sender of the message only.

Reply to all recipients of the e-mail group.

What Do They Do On-Line?

Excerpts from an article by Jared Sandberg. Reprinted by permission of The Wall Street Journal, *December 9, 1996, copyright 1996 Dow Jones & Company, Inc. All rights reserved worldwide.*

Kenneth V. Smith, a 56-year old telecommuter from Sacramento, spends a good chunk of his day on-line—"mostly for work." Or so he says.

True, Mr. Smith, managing editor at a real-estate news service, keeps in touch with the office via e-mail and swaps electronic spreadsheets in seconds. But on a recent day he also booked tickets for his recent trip to San Diego (where he took the trolley to Tijuana after finding out about it on the Internet). And Mr. Smith regularly exchanges messages with his son in New York and daughter in Texas.

But that's not all. "Come to think of it," he adds, he just ordered a mystery novel on-line because "Barnes & Noble didn't have it."

Quietly the World Wide Web is becoming an institution—so quietly, in fact, that a lot of users are astonished when they realize how much they actually do on-line. For many people, the Internet has subsumed the functions of libraries, telephones, televisions, catalogs—even support groups and singles bars. And that's just a sample of its capabilities.

"This thing on our desk swallows the telephone, swallows the fax machine and winds up being the place where we integrate all our communications and publishing," says Jerry Michalski, editor of the high-tech newsletter Release 1.0. "We're only now beginning to uncover the range of possibilities."

That concept is mind-boggling, considering just how much stuff is *already* out there. Search for the phrase "the meaning of life" and you can't imagine how many Internuts have taken a stab—and not much more than that—at answering the question. One search engine provides a list of 2,713,082 sites that address the issue in their own way. . . .

Most people put the Net's enormous resources to more pragmatic use. Margaret Walker, a business student at the University of South Carolina, bypasses the library for the Internet to find back issues of financial magazines for her economics class.

"You don't have to go to the library and spend hours reading stuff when you can type in a search phrase and let [a search engine] do the work," says Ms. Walker, who also can't resist the ease of shopping electronically. She buys her flowers from the 1-800-Flowers site on America Online, uses the service's travel features to plan her vacations and buys everything from compact discs to a fancy nightgown from Web outlets. "I prefer to shop on-line," she says. "It's less crowded."

But e-mail remains the most popular on-line application. By one estimate, 400 million e-mail messages speed through the Internet each day. And, as of July, 32% of the 13.5 million on-line households mentioned e-mail as the primary personal use of cyberspace, compared with only 21% six months earlier, according to a survey by San Francisco-based researchers Odyssey Ventures Inc.

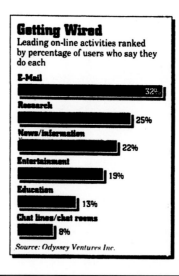

Getting Wired
Leading on-line activities ranked by percentage of users who say they do each

E-Mail 32%
Research 25%
News/information 22%
Entertainment 19%
Education 13%
Chat lines/chat rooms 8%

Source: Odyssey Ventures Inc.

Introduction to the World Wide Web

In this project, you will learn about the World Wide Web and some features that are used to enhance its functionality and appeal.

Objectives

After completing this project, you will be able to do the following:

➤ **Understand the history and use of the World Wide Web**

➤ **Evaluate World Wide Web browsers**

The Challenge

You have been assigned the task of putting together a presentation about the World Wide Web for your supervisor and co-workers. During this presentation, you will need to explain what the World Wide Web is and how it can be a useful tool for Wildlife Rescue International employees, volunteers, and contacts.

The Solution

In this project, you will learn about the World Wide Web and some of the features that enhance it. You will also use the different WWW browsers and choose one for WRI.

Understanding the World Wide Web

The World Wide Web, also known as the Web or WWW, is the Internet service that has revolutionized communications in the 1990s. Prior to the early '90s, university staff, government employees, and military personnel who were doing research or had computer expertise were the only people who used the Internet extensively. Now millions of users are surfing the Web and even publishing their own Web pages.

In 1989, Tim Berners-Lee at CERN, the European Laboratory for Particle Physics in Geneva, Switzerland, developed a new set of standards for exchanging information on the Internet. The World Wide Web provided a way to link documents on any computer on any network. The release in 1992 of the World Wide Web standard, based on public specifications, allowed everyone to develop applications.

As its name implies, the World Wide Web is a collection of documents on computers all over the world. They are connected to each other by hypertext links. That is, you click on hypertext or a "hot" spot in the document, and you are transferred to the linked document. Hypertext, which is the hot text, contains the invisible address of the computer where the linked document resides, and generally appears underlined and in a different color from the surrounding text. You use **HTML**, **HyperText Markup Language**, to create Web documents that contain hyperlinks.

You need **browser** software to find and process the hypertext links. A Web document is a page of plain text and formatting that the browser interprets and renders into a page. The formatting is performed using Hyper-Text Markup Language (HTML), which adds formatting codes to the text. You cannot see the codes in finished Web pages because the browser has translated them into modified text. For instance, a Web page may have the words "Wildlife Rescue International" at the top. The HTML page that contains the codes for the finished Web page may have codes around that text that tell the browser to show it in large, bold letters. The Web browser reads in those coded requests and performs the appropriate actions to make the text "Wildlife Rescue International" appear large and bold. The early browsers were text based. In 1993, the National Center for Super-computing Applications (NCSA) released Mosaic, developed by Marc Andreessen and others at the University of Illinois at Champaign-Urbana. Mosaic was the first graphical Web browser, allowing users to click the mouse not only on text, but also on graphics and icons. Since the release of the first graphical browser, the Web has become the communications phenomenon of the late twentieth century with business and individuals wanting a presence on the Web.

This linking of any document to any other document on the Web allows for nonlinear, nonsequential communications. That is, rather than having to progress through information one page after another as you do with a book, you can browse through the information by clicking on hypertext links or hypermedia (which includes video and audio clips) in the document. In this way, you can read the information in any order rather than in a predefined order.

The information on the Web resides on host computers known as **Web servers**. As mentioned before, the computer on your desk, from which you access information on the World Wide Web or the Internet in general, is known as the **client**.

The client computer that is running a browser requests the linked document. The protocol that enables the transfer of the request and the subsequent transfer of the linked document is **HyperText Transfer Protocol (HTTP)**.

The address of a document, known as its **Uniform Resource Locator (URL)**, looks like the following address for the White House:

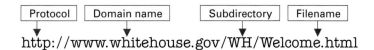

In this example, *http:* names the protocol used and tells the browser how to deal with the document. The protocol is usually separated from the second part, the domain name, with two forward slashes (/). The domain name often, but not necessarily, begins with the three characters *www* to signify that the document is on a Web server. The last section of the URL (preceded by the first single forward slash) is the path or folder (directory) on the server where the file is located. Subfolders or subdirectories may be part of this path. The file name of the desired file is the last item of the URL. If no file name is specified, the URL refers to the default file in that folder.

The example just cited tells the browser to use the Hypertext Transfer Protocol to transfer the document that is located on the host computer www.whitehouse.gov in the folder WH with the file name Welcome. The document is a hypertext document (ending with the extension .html).

 Tip Because URLs are case sensitive, you must type upper- and lowercase characters carefully. Also be sure to include the punctuation exactly, and never include spaces.

The document that appears on the client's screen is called the **home page**, which is simply the top or first page in a Web document.

TASK 1: TO PRACTICE USING THE WORLD WIDE WEB AND HYPERLINKS

1 Start the browser software, and connect to the World Wide Web.

2 Visit the Computer Museum, the IRS, the White House, CNN news, and other locations by typing the following URLs:

http://www.tcm.org/
http://www.irs.ustreas.gov/
http://www.whitehouse.gov/WH/Welcome.html
http://www.cnn.com/
http://www.shuttle.nasa.gov/

Be careful when you type the addresses; they are case sensitive, and spaces aren't allowed. (These addresses were accurate as of the printing of this book, but the Internet is a constantly changing entity. If you can't contact one of these sites, consult your instructor. Also remember that Web servers may go down, which would cause you to have access problems.)

3 Click on some of the links at each site to connect to other documents on the Web.

Evaluating Browser Software

The computer must have browser software to access documents on the Web. The Web server transfers the information to the browser, and then the connection is broken. Each request by the client computer using a browser requires a new, separate connection to the Web server. This method requires less processing power from the server than a dumb terminal connection would require. Dumb terminals have no computing ability but, rather, just sit with an open connection to their server and either input to or receive information from the server.

Another useful browser feature is the *cache*. The cache is where browsers keep a copy of recently visited pages. When you decide to return to that page, the document is loaded very quickly from your computer's own memory rather than from the distant Web server. There are two types of caches: a place in random access memory (RAM) or a location on the hard disk drive. If the cache your browser uses is in RAM, the memory is cleared when you exit from the browser. If the cache your browser uses is on the hard disk drive, the files are cleared from the cache after a certain period of time, or you can delete them manually.

Each browser displays Web documents in its own way because they each interpret the HTML codes a little differently. That is, someone using Mosaic will see a home page displayed differently than someone using Netscape

Navigator. Figures 3.1 and 3.2 display Microsoft's home page, or main introductory page, using Mosaic and Netscape Navigator, respectively. Note the differences in the presentation of the same page by the different browsers.

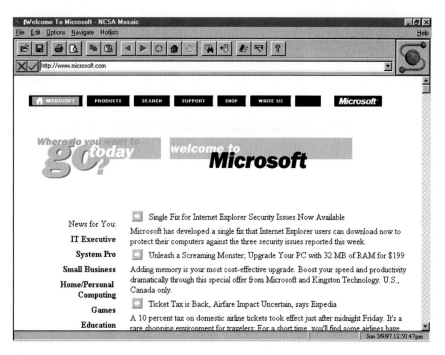

Figure 3.1

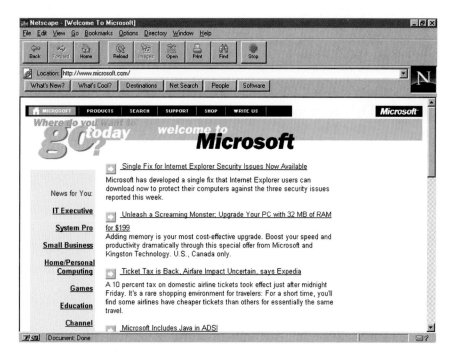

Figure 3.2

The first generation of text browsers is rapidly being replaced by a second generation of graphical browsers. All these newer browsers allow you to click on links and then to move back to the previously displayed page or move back to the opening page. Browsers allow you to open files by typing in the correct URL, print Web documents, and download files. Additionally, browsers allow you to set **bookmarks**, or **favorites**, to mark home pages to which you want to return. (Figure 3.3 shows a list of bookmarks set by one user.) Bookmarks are maintained by the browser even after you turn off the computer.

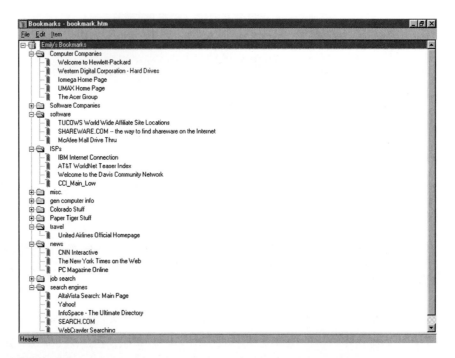

Figure 3.3

 Tip Use bookmarks and favorites to keep track of Web sites that you visit often. You can organize bookmarks by topic by using folders like those in the Windows Explorer File Manager if you use Windows 95. Check in the menu listings at the top of the browser to find the option for organizing these listings. You can create topic folders and then click and drag the listings into them.

Loading home pages with graphics can be slow, so you might want to speed up the process by not taking the time to load graphics. You don't have to use a different browser; you can simply set the graphical browser to load pages as text only.

While you're online, the browser maintains a *history list* of the last Web pages that you visited. By using this list, you can quickly move to a document directly rather than move back one page at a time by using the Back button in the browser. (Figure 3.4 shows a history list of visited sites.)

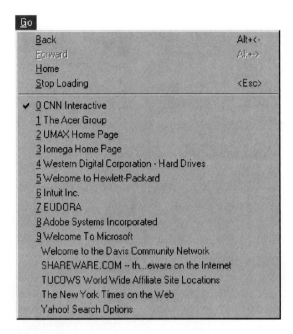

Figure 3.4

Many home pages contain forms into which you can enter information. The browser displays the form (like the one shown in Figure 3.5), takes the data that you type into the form, and sends an e-mail message that contains the contents of the form to the person requesting it or places that information in a database.

Please give us your comments and/or suggestions

Restrict comments to **web page design and organization topics** only. If you need **HELP** or a **REPLY** from us, please use the Help Desk page.

Name:

Email:

Geography you most often access from: North America

Send Feedback   Clear Form

Figure 3.5

The three most popular browsers are Mosaic, Netscape Navigator, and Microsoft Internet Explorer.

Currently, NCSA Mosaic 2.1.1 is the latest version of the first graphical browser. You can find the home page for Mosaic, which is shown in Figure 3.6, at `http://www.ncsa.uiuc.edu/SDG/Software/WinMosaic/HomePage.html`. Mosaic has some nice features, such as AutoSurf, which automatically follows links and saves them on the client's hard disk drive for viewing offline. However, Mosaic's popularity has fallen off in the last few years.

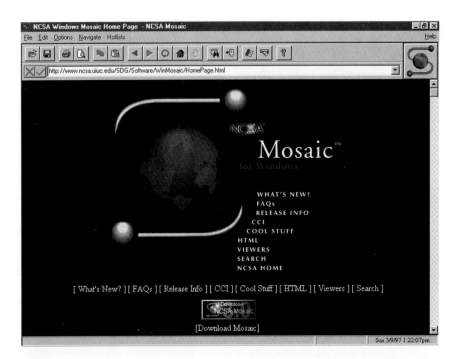

Figure 3.6

Netscape Navigator 3.0 has two versions: Atlas and Atlas Gold. The Atlas Gold version includes a Web page editor for creating your own Web documents. You can find the home page for Netscape Navigator, which is shown in Figure 3.7, at `http://home.netscape.com`. Currently, Netscape is the most popular Web browser—claiming 85 percent of the browser market—and has been called the most popular PC application of all time. Netscape provides great flexibility with ***plug-ins***—software applications that expand a browser's basic capabilities by actually becoming an extension of the browser itself. Plug-ins are different from ***helper applications,*** which are completely separate programs that the browser opens upon request for your convenience. You can think of a plug-in as a non-essential addition to a Web browser's functions. Like a spelling checker in an e-mail program, it's a helpful and wonderful feature but you could live without it. A helper application is opened by the browser like an application that is launched from an e-mail program. You click on a certain icon or highlighted text in the browser and the associated program is opened. The various plug-ins and helper applications allow you to participate in activities such as chatting with other users or signing documents on the Web by

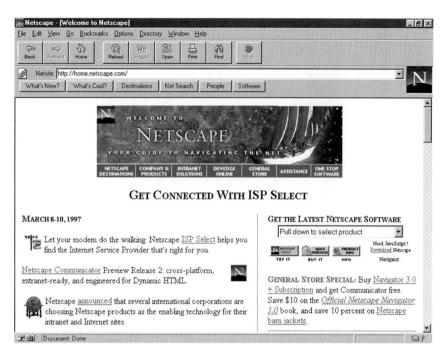

Figure 3.7

using a digitizing pad. Netscape includes e-mail, newsgroup readers, and File Transfer Protocol (FTP). The last two topics will be discussed in Projects 6* and 7*, respectively.

Microsoft Internet Explorer for Windows 95 is becoming very popular with Windows 95 users. (You can find the Internet Explorer home page, which is shown in Figure 3.8, at `http://www.microsoft.com/ie/default.asp`.

Figure 3.8

Internet Explorer also includes e-mail, news programs, FTP, plug-ins, and helper applications. Because it comes as part of Windows 95, it is rapidly expanding its user base especially for first-time users. However, some security holes have been discovered by users. You can fix these bugs by logging into the Microsoft Web site and downloading the files that plug the security holes.

There is stiff competition between Netscape and Microsoft to produce the most popular Web browser. Therefore, there is a high turnover rate for each product as the two companies constantly roll out "new and improved" versions of their software. You can look forward to more advanced products that will eventually cover all of your Internet needs from e-mail to live chatting.

TASK 2: TO EVALUATE BROWSER SOFTWARE FOR WRI

1 Go through steps 1 through 10 individually for Mosaic, Netscape Navigator, and Internet Explorer.

2 Open the browser.

3 Type in the URL **http://www.microsoft.com**.

4 Save the site using a bookmark or favorite.

5 Type in the URL **http://home.netscape.com**.

6 Use the back arrow to go back to Microsoft's home page.

7 Use the forward arrow to go back to Netscape's home page.

8 Type in the URL

http://www.ncsa.uiuc.edu/SDG/Software/WinMosaic/HomePage.html.

9 View the history list.

10 Go back to each of the three home pages, and familiarize yourself with the browser by navigating through the sites.

11 After you complete the preceding 10 steps for each of the browsers, based on the ease of use of each Web browser and the way they present the Web pages, decide on a Web browser for WRI's use.

12 Open a word processing program.

13 Type **Choosing a World Wide Web Browser** for the header.

14 Type the name of your chosen browser, and write a short paragraph describing the reasons you chose this browser over the other two.

15 Save the document as WWW.doc, and close the word processing program.

Because the World Wide Web has grown so rapidly, and millions of documents now exist all over the world on every topic you can imagine, finding the information you want can be a challenge. You can use the browser to connect to a *search engine*, which is software that helps you find information. Because it is such an important topic, Project 4, "Searching the

World Wide Web," is entirely dedicated to the discussion of searching the Internet.

Conclusion

This concludes Project 3. Review your work, read the summary below, and do the following exercises.

Summary and Exercises

Summary

- The World Wide Web is a web of documents on computers all over the world. They are linked by hypertext
- Software known as a browser is needed to find and process the hypertext links.
- Graphical browsers allow you to click on text and graphics or icons to link to other locations.
- Hypertext Transfer Protocol (HTTP) is the protocol that is used to transfer the Web documents.
- The Uniform Resource Locator (URL) is an address that pinpoints a document on the World Wide Web.
- The cache is used to store recently visited sites on your personal computer so they can be quickly loaded when you request to visit them again.
- A home page is the main page on a Web site.
- You can use bookmarks or favorites to organize a listing of frequently visited Web sites.
- A history list contains the URLs of the most recently visited Web sites.
- Plug-ins are small programs that extend the functionality of the Web browser.
- The Web browser calls upon helper applications to run a program external to itself.

Key Terms

bookmarks	home page
browser	Hypertext Markup Language (HTML)
cache	Hypertext Transfer Protocol (HTTP)
client	plug-ins
dumb terminals	search engine
favorites	Uniform Resource Locator (URL)
helper applications	Web server
history list	

Study Questions

Multiple Choice

1. The World Wide Web is
   a. a network of computers.
   b. an Internet service.
   c. a protocol.
   d. the oldest part of the Internet.
   e. a network of telephone lines.

2. Hypertext is
   a. used to link documents.
   b. a search engine.
   c. requires a plug-in to be viewed by a browser.
   d. forces the visitor to view Web pages like a book.
   e. includes sound and video.

3. Browsers
    a. are software.
    b. are needed to find and process the hypertext links.
    c. have changed from being only text based to include graphics.
    d. such as Netscape Navigator have become very popular.
    e. all the above.

4. Web documents are
    a. sequential.
    b. linear.
    c. nonsequential.
    d. repetitive.
    e. circular.

5. HTTP
    a. is a programming language.
    b. stands for HyperTelnet Transfer Protocol.
    c. stands for Hypertext Transfer Protocol.
    d. is a plug-in standard.
    e. is used to transfer sound.

6. The URL http://www.cyberpanda.com/panda/help.html
    a. includes a Word document.
    b. requires a helper application to be viewed.
    c. contains the domain name cyberpanda.com.
    d. uses the File Transfer Protocol.
    e. does not include a folder on the server.

7. The URL http://www.cyberpanda.com/panda/help.html
    a. calls on the protocol "cyberpanda.com"
    b. calls on the protocol "panda"
    c. calls on the protocol "help"
    d. calls on the protocol "http"
    e. calls on the protocol "html"

8. A cache
    a. is the address to locate a Web page
    b. is a built-in program to the Web browser
    c. organizes your favorite web sites.
    d. stores recently visited web sites.
    e. is a list of the search engines you visit most.

9. URLs
    a. are Internet protocols
    b. are Web page addresses
    c. list recently visited sites
    d. none of the above
    e. all of the above

10. What helps you organize URLs for frequently visited sites by allowing you to create topic folders?
   a. caches
   b. favorites
   c. history lists
   d. helper applications
   e. plug-ins

Short Answer

   http://wwf.org/species/index.html

1. What is the name of the file in the preceding URL?

2. What is the protocol in the preceding URL?

3. What type of server does the preceding URL point to?

4. How do bookmarks help you organize?

5. Define what a browser does.

6. Define URL.

7. What is HTTP?

8. What is HTML?

9. What is a helper application?

10. What is a plug-in?

For Discussion

1. Explain how browsers display their content.

2. How are the caching methods different?

3. How are dumb terminals different from Web browsers?

4. Explain how Web documents are different from books.

5. What is the purpose of forms in a Web page?

Review Exercises

1. Reviewing the history of the World Wide Web
Based on what you learned in this project, summarize the history of the WWW in one short paragraph. Also summarize the following terms in one sentence each: hypertext, hypermedia, browser, URL, Web server, client, HTTP.

2. Understanding Browsers
Describe browsers by summarizing the following terms in one sentence each: cache, home page, bookmarks, history list, plug-ins, helper applications.

Assignments

1. Using the World Wide Web
In your browser software, type in the following URL:

http://www.e-cards.com/

Follow the directions to send an e-mail postcard to a friend.

2. Setting a Bookmark
In your browser software, set a bookmark at the following site:

http://www.nps.gov/

Visit another site, and then use bookmarks or favorites to return to the National Park Service page.

How Can You Make Money from the Web?

Excerpts from an article by William M. Bulkeley. Reprinted by permission of The Wall Street Journal, *December 9, 1996, copyright 1996 Dow Jones & Company, Inc. All rights reserved worldwide.*

So far, many entrepreneurs lament, the only way to make a small fortune on the Internet has been to start with a large one.

Sure, businesspeople and investors are cashing in big on building the Internet, or providing access to it—witness the success of companies such as browser maker Netscape Communications Corp. or Cisco Systems Inc., with its router switches.

But what about people who don't write software code, build computers or own phone lines? After all, the prime commercial allure of the Internet is supposed to be that its ubiquity and speed can help people make money the old-fashioned way: by selling goods or services.

For this bunch, costs have been high, and profits elusive. A recent survey by International Data Corp., Framingham, Mass., found companies are paying an average of $1 million to build World Wide Web sites. For most players, that's a high entry cost. . . .

Herewith, some lessons from businesses that have hung on:

- Get businesses to pay, not the consumer.
- Web surfers are bargain hunters.
- Offer a huge selection.
- Don't quit your day job; Web-link it.
- Branch out.
- Insert yourself in the transaction chain.
- Let someone else do the dirty work.
- Selling subscriptions is a get-rich-slow formula.

PROJECT

Searching the World Wide Web

In this project, you will learn to search for information on the World Wide Web. You will learn to use various search tools and to limit your search with those tools, finding the specific information you need.

Objectives

After completing this project, you will be able to do the following:

➤ **Search the Web for information**

➤ **Search for information using a directory or index service**

➤ **Search for information using a search engine**

➤ **Search for information using a specialized directory**

➤ **Understand cookie technology**

The Challenge

Wildlife Rescue International needs to find specific information about animals that is located on the World Wide Web. For example, you have been asked to find specific information on the migration patterns of the sandhill crane.

The Solution

You search the Web for information on migration of the sandhill crane and locate the Spring Migration Guide, as shown in Figure 4.1.

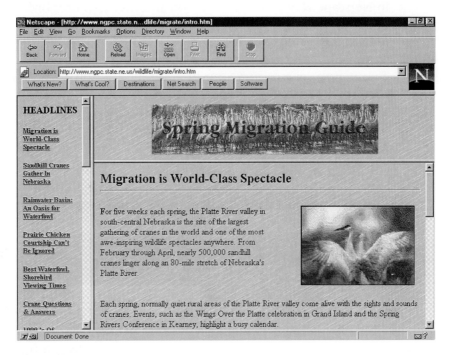

Figure 4.1

Finding Information on the World Wide Web

Finding information on the World Wide Web can be like looking for a needle in a haystack. Although searching on the WWW can be extremely frustrating at times, it can also be so interesting and fun that you can lose track of time and spend many hours searching. In fact, searching on the WWW can take so much time and be so enjoyable that employers are finding ways to monitor employees who surf the Web on the job.

Because finding the correct information in a timely manner is important, many companies have created search tools to help you with your searches. You will use many of these search tools in this project.

Searching the Web

To find specific information on a topic, you must either know the exact URL, or you must use a *search tool*, which is software designed to help you find information among the millions of documents on the World Wide Web. Most available search tools are free because they include advertising on nearly every page. Some of the most popular search services include Yahoo!, Magellan, Infoseek, Excite, Lycos, AltaVista, WebCrawler, and Dogpile. You can find these search services by using a special feature in Netscape Navigator or Microsoft Internet Explorer or by manually typing the URL of the particular service you want to use into the URL address field of your Web browser.

To initiate a search from your browser, you simply click on the Net Search button in Netscape Navigator or on the Search button in Internet Explorer. You are presented with a page that links you to search tools, that is, the **search engines** and **directories**. For example, when you click the Net Search button in Netscape Navigator, you see a screen similar to Figure 4.2 in which miniaturized versions of the search tools are displayed.

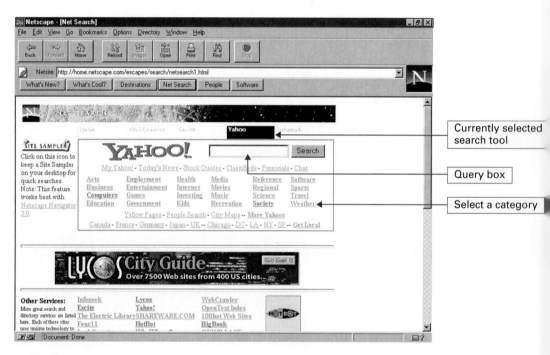

Figure 4.2

The currently selected search tool has a black tab. You can then select one of the other search tools by clicking on its tab, or you can use the currently selected tool. You can use different types of tools for different types of searches. For example, if you know exactly what you're looking for or at least have a good idea, then you should use a directory or **index**. These search tools are developed by people who research sites and manually enter **keywords** about those sites into databases. However, if you want to see what is available on the Internet, you should use a search engine, which indexes every word on a page by using specialized software.

Using Directories or Indexes

Internet directories are catalogs or indexes of Web sites compiled by researchers whose job is to create databases. These databases don't always list every Web site on a topic; instead, the researchers compiling the database include only relevant sites and often rate sites for their relevancy to your search. To use a directory, you narrow your search by choosing categories that are arranged in hierarchies. For example, using *Yahoo!* (http://www.yahoo.com), one of the most popular directories, to find societies or organizations whose purpose is to protect manatees, you would select the following categories one level at a time from the hierarchy: Society/Animal Rights/Endangered Species/Manatees.

Then from the resulting list, you could choose Duval County Manatee Research Grant to view the Web document, as shown in Figure 4.3.

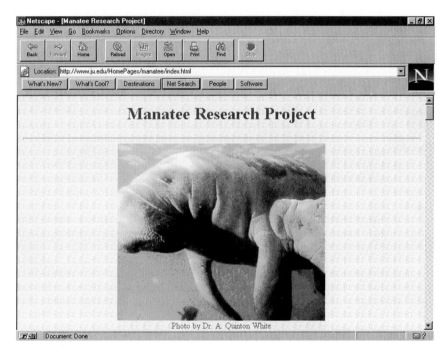

Figure 4.3   http://www.ju.edu/HomePages/manatee/index.html

If you want to find organizations whose purpose is to protect whales, and you notice that none are listed on the endangered species page, you would choose the following categories one at a time from the hierarchy: Society/Animal Rights/Endangered Species. Then you would type the keyword **whales** into the *query box*, the text box provided by the search site.

Keywords, which you type in the query box, are the words that the search tool, such as Yahoo!, matches in the database. Before displaying the results of the search, Yahoo! sorts the results according to relevancy; that is, the highest ranked documents appear first in the list. For example, documents with the keyword in the title are ranked higher than documents with the keyword only in the body of the document. Also, if you're searching for multiple keywords, documents that contain all the keywords are ranked higher than documents that contain only some of the keywords.

 Tip Each search tool contains online help to help you narrow your search.

To help you narrow your directory search in Yahoo!, use the following tips:

- Use double quotation marks around words that should be considered a phrase. For example, by placing quotation marks around **"Pacific Humpback whales"**, you find only results that match the words in the exact sequence.
- Place a plus sign in front of words that must be found in every search result. Placing a plus sign in front of *tiger* in **+Siberian+Tiger** requires that the word *tiger* be found in all results; therefore, you don't get *Siberian Husky* matches.
- Place a minus sign in front of words that must not be found in your search results. Placing a minus sign in front of *island* in **+Kodiak+bear-island** requires that search results containing the words *Kodiak Island* would not appear in the resulting list of matches.

 Tip When typing in text to search for, don't include spaces between the words if you are including an operator such as the plus sign (+), and be careful of making words plural because it will result in the word only appearing as plural in the hits.

The results of searches are called ***hits***. You can see the total number of hits that resulted, but usually only the first 10 or 20 hits are displayed along with a brief description of the site. If more hits result, you can click on an option to display the next group of results if you don't find what you want in the first group. The list of results contains hyperlinks to corresponding sites, so you can simply click the link to be transferred to a site.

TASK 1: TO USE THE DIRECTORY YAHOO! TO SEARCH FOR INFORMATION

1 Start your browser and connect to the World Wide Web.

2 Type the URL **http://www.yahoo.com** and press (ENTER), or click the Net Search button and select Yahoo! if it isn't already displayed.

3 Use the directories and keyword searches to help Wildlife Rescue International locate information on the following topics:

Kenya's black rhinoceros
Galapagos Islands
whooping cranes
scarlet macaws
lowland gorillas

Infoseek, another popular directory service, claims the motto "proof of intelligent life on the net," as you can see in Figure 4.4.

Figure 4.4   http://www.infoseek.com

You use this service by typing the words you want to search in the query box. Then you select the type of documents you want to search, such as newsgroups, news stories from the past month, the news for the current day, a database of addresses for a specific e-mail address, or company profiles. You also can search the entire Web. Infoseek displays the results, along with related topics. If you received too many hits, you can further refine your search, or if your search was too narrow, you can expand your search. The following tips will help you search the Infoseek directory:

● Words that appear next to each other and are capitalized are considered as a single name—for example, **Harrison Ford** is one name.
● Words that appear with commas between them are considered separately—for example, **Harrison, Ford** is two names.
● Use quotation marks around or hyphens between words that should be considered as one—for example, **"tropical rain forest"** or **tropical-rain-forest**.
● Use the plus sign in front of words that must appear in results and a minus sign in front of words that must not appear in results—just as described for Yahoo!.
● Use a pipe symbol (|) to narrow your search to a word, and then search for a word in that category—for example, **whales | baleen**.

By using advanced searches in Infoseek, you can search for words in the title of a document, for words contained in the URL, and for hypertext links to a certain page. Use the Infoseek help or tip feature for advanced searches.

Using Search Engines

Search engines, the second main category of search tools, search for the keyword or words you type into the query box and find documents that contain the words. Search engines use software called **spiders**, **webcrawlers**, or **robots** that compile databases of references to keywords. Then, when you initiate a search using a search engine, your keyword is matched to words in the database, and the documents that contain references to these words are listed for you. Many of the directory services have agreements with search engines to help your search. For example, if you don't find what you're looking for when using Yahoo!, you are prompted by Yahoo! to use AltaVista, which is a search engine.

Because so many documents are available on the Internet, and your keywords may be contained in so many of them, narrowing your search can be very important. Each search engine has its own way of searching, and each provides search tips and online help to aid your searches. Using a search engine's advanced searching capabilities involves **Boolean logic**. George Boole, a nineteenth-century mathematician, applied mathematical symbols to logic to help clarify and simplify logical relationships. Boolean logic has been used extensively with computer programs and databases. You also can use this logic to help with searches. To do so, you can limit your searches by linking two keywords with AND, or you can expand your search by linking keywords with OR.

 Caution You must enter Boolean operators in all caps when typing them into a query box.

Table 4.1 describes Boolean operators.

Table 4.1

Operator	Function	Example
AND	Documents must contain all words joined with AND.	To find *gorillas*, *mist*, and *movie*, enter **gorillas AND mist AND movie**.
OR	Documents found must contain at least one of the words joined with OR.	To find *humpback* or *baleen* whales, enter **humpback OR baleen**.
NOT	Documents found can't contain the word that follows NOT.	To find *Siberian tigers*, not *Siberian huskies*, enter **Siberian AND tiger NOT husky**.

 Tip Each search engine has specific syntax for entering advanced searches, so you should always check the online help for search tips.

WebCrawler, shown in Figure 4.5, is one of the most popular search engines; it searches an index of the World Wide Web that is updated daily. WebCrawler's logo pictures Spidy the spider, who tells you to "Search before you surf!"

Figure 4.5 http://www.webcrawler.com

Along with the Boolean operators described in Table 4.1, WebCrawler provides the operators described in Table 4.2 for advanced searches.

Table 4.2

Operator	Function	Example
NEAR	The two words must appear next to each other.	**Endangered NEAR species**
NEAR/XX	The two words must appear within *XX* words of each other. Simply replace the *XX* with the number you want.	**Tropical NEAR/30 forest**
"..."	The words in quotation marks must be in the designated order.	**"tropical rain forest"**
(...)	Parentheses are used to clarify complex searches.	**robin NOT(Williams OR Christopher)**

Other WebCrawler features include using city maps, searching to see who has links to your home page, and checking out popular sites.

AltaVista, another popular search engine, allows both simple and complex searches. Figure 4.6 shows this engine.

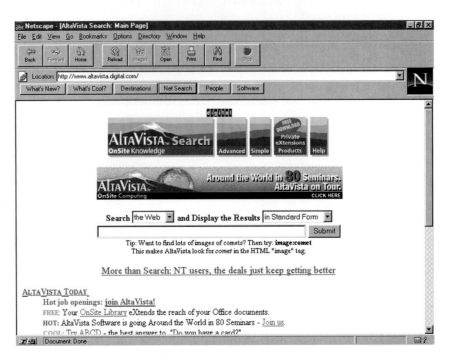

Figure 4.6   http://www.altavista.digital.com

AltaVista indexes all words in a Web document and uses the first few words as a short abstract that is displayed as part of the search results. Words are designated by AltaVista as any group of characters surrounded by punctuation, white space, or nonalphabetic characters, allowing you to find text that does not appear in any dictionary.

AltaVista uses the operators AND, OR, NOT, and NEAR in the same way described for WebCrawler; however, the NEAR operator finds only instances of the two words within 10 words of each other.

Using advanced queries in AltaVista, you can see documents that are ranked; that is, a document with a high score has the word you search for located in the first few words of the document, or it contains the word more than once. In AltaVista, you can also limit searches to portions of documents, such as titles, URLs, anchors, links, or even names of images. Use AltaVista help for these advanced searches.

TASK 2: TO USE THE SEARCH ENGINE ALTAVISTA TO SEARCH FOR INFORMATION

1 Start your browser and connect to the World Wide Web.

2 Type the URL **http://www.altavista.digital.com** and press ⏎ENTER⏎, or click the Net Search button and select AltaVista if it isn't already displayed.

3 Search for the following:

killer whales
tiger NEAR lion
endangered elephants
endangered marine mammals

Excite, shown in Figure 4.7, is another popular search engine.

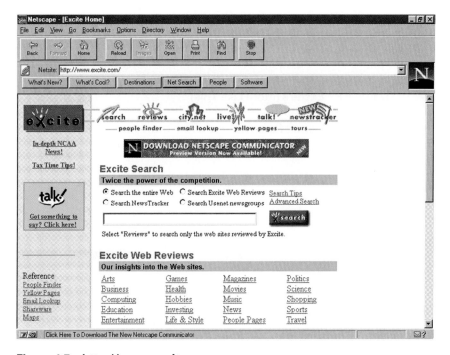

Figure 4.7   http://www.excite.com

Excite, like other search engines, looks for documents containing the exact words entered in the query box; however, it also expands your search by looking for ideas that are closely related to the words you entered. For example, if you enter the words **"saving wildlife and habitats"**, you not only find exact matches for the text, but you also find sites mentioning conservation and endangered species. Excite's search engine makes relationships between words in a document that mean the same thing. When Excite displays the hits that match your criteria, it also displays the clickable option *More Like This*, as you can see in Figure 4.8, for you to find more results related to your search.

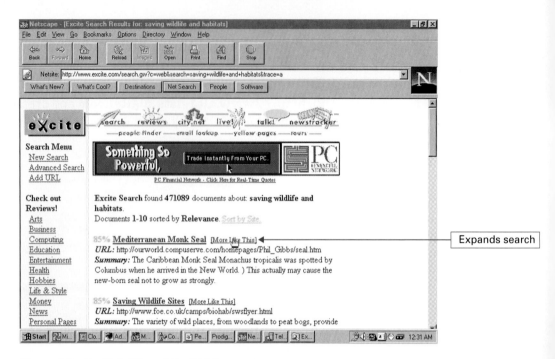

Figure 4.8   Excite's [More Like This]

Excite also combines the use of human researchers with its search engine to review thousands of sites for quality, helping your search to result in quality sites.

HotBot, another popular search engine, calls itself "The wired search engine." Figure 4.9 shows this search engine in action.

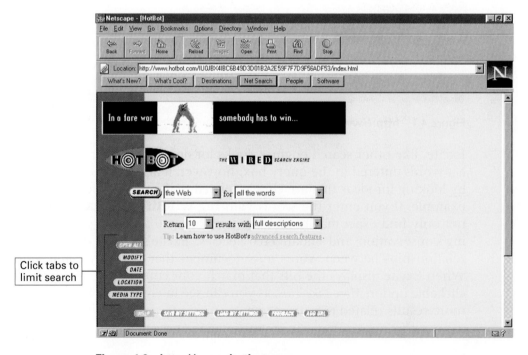

Figure 4.9   http://www.hotbot.com

HotBot provides a simple interface. You simply tell HotBot where to search and for what words. Then you follow down the screen and limit the search results by adjusting how many results you want to see and whether you want full descriptions. You can modify the search by selecting words that must be contained in the search or words that must not be contained in the results. You can also limit the time frame for the search under the Date section, the location of the document geographically or physically under the Location section, and the type of document or media type.

Lycos provides searching capabilities in the following areas: the entire Web, for sites by subject, for sound, and for pictures. Other services include top news stories, top 5 percent of reviewed sites, a people finder, road maps, and a city guide.

Lycos, shown in Figure 4.10, is another powerful search engine.

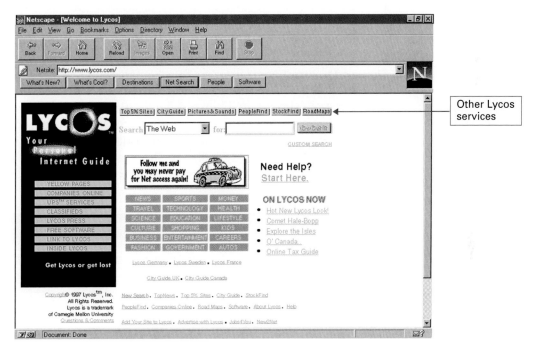

Figure 4.10   http://www.lycos.com

Using Specialized Directories

You can find specific information such as information on a company, government agency, a person's address or phone number, or a toll-free number in specialized directories. Click the Net search button on your browser and then scroll down the screen, as shown in Figure 4.11, to see a list of these directories.

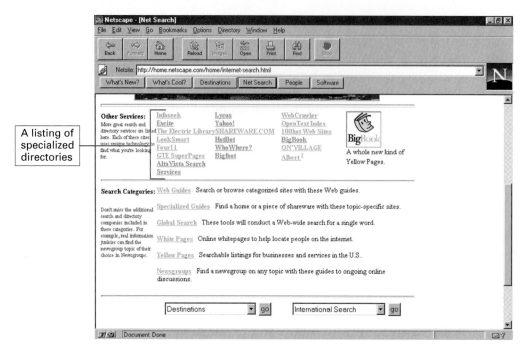

A listing of specialized directories

Figure 4.11   http://home.netscape.com/home/internet-search.html

WhoWhere?, shown in Figure 4.12, is a specialized directory providing e-mail addresses for people on the Internet, phone numbers and addresses for over 90 million U.S. residential phone listings, toll-free numbers for over 300,000 businesses, online yellow pages, and URLs for companies, U.S. government agencies, and individuals.

Select to limit search

Figure 4.12   http://www.whowhere.com

Also if you want to find someone and know the school he or she attends or attended or groups he or she belongs to, then WhoWhere? can help you locate that person. Select WhoWhere? from the list, or type **http://www. whowhere.com**. Type the person's name and any other information about the person's address such as e-mail provider and then start the search.

Four11 is another specialized directory providing e-mail addresses, telephone numbers, and addresses for government agencies, individuals, and even celebrities.

To use Four11, select it from the list, or type **http://www.four11.com**. Enter as much information as you know about the individual you're looking for and then perform the search.

Another search site that finds addresses and phone listings for businesses is the *BigBook*. Select BigBook from the list, or type **http://www.big-book.com**. BigBook searches over 16 million U.S. business listings. Not only can you search for a business by name, but you also can search by the category and narrow the search by the city and state.

Figure 4.13 shows BigBook's web site.

Figure 4.13   http://www.bigbook.com

Bigfoot, a search site that charges for full service, is both a mail service and a search site for finding e-mail and addresses for individuals, as you can see in Figure 4.14.

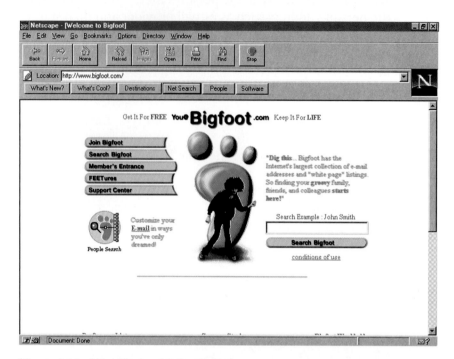

Figure 4.14   http://www.bigfoot.com/

Using Bigfoot, you can search for people by name and narrow the search by including any other information. Simply choose Bigfoot from the list, or type **http://www.bigfoot.com**.

Bigfoot membership also provides you with an e-mail address for life, which ensures consistency and your privacy. For example, even if you change ISPs several times, thus changing your e-mail address, no one would know because your mail is sent to you at YOU@BIGFOOT.COM and is simply forwarded to you at any address you designate. You can retain your privacy, stop unsolicited junk e-mail, and stop direct marketing *snail mail* (mail sent through the post office) using Bigfoot's built-in filtering. You can even receive your Bigfoot e-mail wirelessly on your pager, PCS telephone, or palmtop computer.

TASK 3: TO USE THE SPECIALIZED
SEARCH SITES TO SEARCH FOR INFORMATION

1 Start your browser and connect to the World Wide Web.

2 Use any of the specialized search tools described in this section to find the following:
Your senator's e-mail address
The e-mail address for the U.S. Fish and Wildlife department
World Wildlife Fund's street address
A pet store in your area
A home page for the U.S. Bureau of Land Management

Meta Search Tools

New search tools are being developed all the time. One new type of search tool is the **meta search tool** that searches several other search tools for you. This saves you from having to repeat your search. Examples of meta search tools are MetaCrawler and Dogpile (located at www.dogpile.com.)

MetaCrawler, which is shown in Figure 4.15, is a search service that can save you a great deal of time.

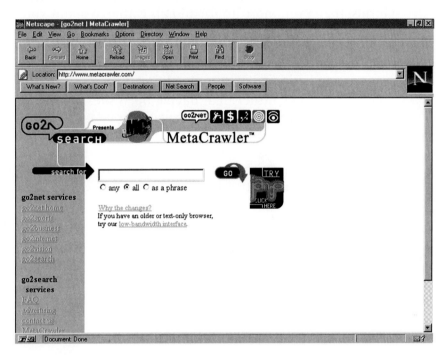

Figure 4.15   http://www.metacrawler.com

You can connect to MetaCrawler by typing **http://www.meta-crawler.com**. On this search site, you can type in the text for which you want to search just as you do with any other search engine; however, MetaCrawler submits your query to multiple search sites at the same time. The results page then shows the results from all the searches at one time, saving you from having to repeat the search numerous times.

What Is Cookie Technology?

Cookies are text files that Web sites you visit store on your computer. The file can include your user name, the date you last visited the Web site, and any other information that the Web site wants to put into the file. When you visit the Web site again, your browser will look for a cookie file on your hard disk drive, and if it finds one, it will send the file to the site. The Web site then uses the information in the cookie file to tailor the information at the Web site to your preferences.

This activity seems harmless and one that might save time. For example, if you visit a site often to get updated information on a certain subject, a cookie file can create a shortcut for you to the information you periodically want.

However handy this concept sounds, though, many people are worried about the privacy and security issues involved. For example, people who feel quite anonymous surfing the Web are surprised to realize that information about the sites they visit and searches they conduct can be saved in files used to create a user profile. And if you fill out user registration forms, then even more information is gathered about you. People are also surprised to find out that Web sites can write to their hard disk drives.

Not only does the cookie technology affect privacy, but it also affects the spirit of the Web. If the future of the Web is having sites customized to your user profile rather than having open sites, you could miss information you want because it is not available to you.

As privacy precautions, you might want to consider what information you make available to Web sites in registration forms, and you might want to turn off the cookie option in your browser.

The Next Step

Practice using the various search tools to find information of interest to you. Compare results of searches using the different tools. Use search tools that were not covered in this project to see what different features they have to offer.

Conclusion

Now that you've completed Project 4, review your work, read the summary, and do the following exercises.

Summary and Exercises

Summary

- Internet directories are catalogs of Web sites compiled by researchers, who include only relevant sites and often rate sites for their relevancy to your search.
- Keywords, which you type in the query box, are the words that the search tool matches in the database
- The results of searches are called hits.
- Search engines search for the keyword or words you type into the query box and find documents that contain the words.
- Search engines use software called spiders, webcrawlers, or robots that compile databases.
- Boolean logic developed by George Boole, a nineteenth-century mathematician, applies mathematical symbols to logic to help clarify and simplify logical relationships.
- Specialized directories serve specific searching needs such as finding e-mail addresses, phone numbers, street addresses, and information on businesses and government agencies.
- Cookies are text files that Web sites you visit store on your computer.

Key Terms

AltaVista	Lycos
BigBook	Metacrawler
Bigfoot	meta search tools
Boolean logic	robots
cookies	search engines
directories	search tool
Excite	snail mail
Four11	spiders
hits	query box
HotBot	WebCrawler
index	webcrawlers
Infoseek	WhoWhere?
keywords	Yahoo!

Study Questions

Multiple Choice

1. A directory
   a. is compiled by a robot.
   b. makes use of spider programs.
   c. is compiled by a human.
   d. is also known as a spelling checker.
   e. is useful if you aren't sure what information you're looking for.

2. A search engine
   a. makes use of spider programs.
   b. relies on keyword searches.
   c. uses Boolean logic.
   d. is useful if you aren't sure what information you're looking for.
   e. all the above.

3. To find information on a particular agency, what is the best tool to use?
   a. a directory
   b. a cookie
   c. a search engine
   d. a specialized directory
   e. all the above

4. Directories list topics
   a. randomly.
   b. ranked by quality.
   c. in hierarchies.
   d. in lists of keywords.
   e. in spiders.

5. Boolean logic
   a. helps limit searches.
   b. has been used extensively by computer programs.
   c. places operators in keywords.
   d. is named for a nineteenth-century mathematician.
   e. all the above.

6. Keywords
   a. must be in all caps.
   b. are typed into the query box.
   c. can never be proper names.
   d. should be vague.
   e. all the above.

7. Cookies
   a. are sweet or cool sites on the Web.
   b. deliver sweet messages to friends.
   c. are text files created by Web sites and stored on your hard disk drive.
   d. help you retain privacy on the Internet.
   e. all the above.

8. What is an example of a search engine?
   a. Yahoo!
   b. Magellan
   c. Bigfoot
   d. WebCrawler
   e. all the above

9. What is an example of a directory service?
   a. Yahoo!
   b. Netscape
   c. WebCrawler
   d. Bigfoot
   e. all the above

10. To have the phrase *Endangered Species Act* treated as one entity for searching, you
   a. place asterisks around the phrase.
   b. place quotation marks around the phrase.
   c. place dollar signs around the phrase.
   d. place parentheses around the phrase.
   e. place brackets around the phrase.

Short Answer

1. Place the operators or punctuation marks necessary to find the following:

   tigers in the same document as *lions*

2. Place the operators or punctuation marks necessary to find the following:

   tigers close to *lions* in the same document

3. Place the operators or punctuation marks necessary to find the following:

   tigers but not *lions* in a document

4. Place the operators or punctuation marks necessary to find the following:

   tigers or *lions* in a document

5. Place the operators or punctuation marks necessary to find the following:

   Galapagos Island turtles as one phrase

6. Place the operators or punctuation marks necessary to find the following:

   coral reefs next to each other

7. Place the operators or punctuation marks necessary to find the following:

   China's giant pandas as a phrase

8. Place the operators or punctuation marks necessary to find the following:

   elephant ivory ban near each other

9. Place the operators or punctuation marks necessary to find the following:

   Jane Goodall as a name

10. Place the operators or punctuation marks necessary to find the following:

   blue whale as one entity

For Discussion

1. Discuss privacy issues related to the World Wide Web.

2. Describe Boolean logic.

3. Discuss why it is important to limit searching the Web while on the job.

4. Explain the difference between directory services and search engines.

5. Describe some of your successful and unsuccessful searches of the World Wide Web.

Review Exercises _____

1. **Write the answers to the following questions and the URL where you found the information.**
   1. What date was the Golden Gate Bridge completed and open to pedestrian traffic?

2. What are Ben and Jerry's top three flavors?

3. What are the names of Keiko's (Free Willy's) four trainers?

4. What is one the newest attraction at Universal Studios in Orlando, Florida?

5. What are the top three movies at the box office currently?

6. What is the address of the Hard Rock Café in Cabo San Lucas?

7. Where can a photograph of Madonna be found?

Assignments

1. Using the Map Feature at a Search Site
Find a map of your city. Locate your address and print out the map.

2. Narrowing and Expanding a Search
Choose a topic in which you're interested, such as a breed of dogs. Use a directory and a search engine to search. Print out the results of the search. Repeat the search by narrowing the topic; then print out the results. Repeat the search by broadening the topic; then print out the results.

How Can I Find What I'm Looking For?

Excerpts from an article by Bart Ziegler. Reprinted by permission of The Wall Street Journal, *December 9, 1996, copyright 1996 Dow Jones & Company, Inc. All rights reserved worldwide.*

You are on the Internet, and you want to find something. You access one of the popular services such as AltaVista or Lycos and type in a few search words. A few seconds later, back come the matches—all 20,000 of them.

You've just reached the limitations of search "engines" for the World Wide Web. Indispensable as they are, these sites, though improving, are far from perfect. Designed to help you navigate the vast and ever-growing Web, they can end up leaving you even more bewildered about the new medium.

Web-search services often return thousands of responses to a simple request for information—many of which appear to bear little or no relation to what you are seeking. Moreover, these searches encompass only part of the Web. Most, for instance, don't examine Web sites that require the user to enter a password. That's why a search engine won't find articles that appeared on the sites of the *New York Times* or this newspaper, for instance, or in numerous scientific journals and other specialized sites.

Notes

Notes

Glossary

address books   In an e-mail program, a list of e-mail contacts usually organized by nickname.

ARPAnet (Advanced Research Projects Agency Network)   A network created by the Department of Defense (DOD) in 1969. It linked four universities together —University of California at Los Angeles, Stanford Research Institute, University of California Santa Barbara, and the University of Utah.

Attached   In an e-mail message, this field contains the name of the encoded, attached file.

Attachments   Usually nontext, encoded files that are sent separately from, but attached to, an e-mail message.

backbone operator   An entity that pays for and maintains high-speed lines that link to the major Internet backbone access points.

BCC   Shorthand for Blind Carbon Copy. The field in an e-mail message that is used to send e-mail to people who should be made aware of the information in the e-mail message but to whom the e-mail is not directly addressed. It works just like the *CC:* field in a paper memo; however, the message is sent automatically, and the person named in the TO: field will not know that the e-mail was sent to other people.

BinHex   A method of encoding nontext files. Mostly used by Macintosh systems.

Body   In an e-mail message, this item contains the main text of the message.

Bookmarks   A listing that you create to list sites you visit often or would like to quickly return to. Also known as a "favorite."

Boolean logic   A type of logic created by the nineteenth-century mathematician George Boole. He applied mathematical symbols to logic to help clarify and simplify logical relationships. Boolean logic has been used extensively with computer programs and databases and can help you with your searches. You can limit your searches by linking two keywords with AND, or you can expand your search by linking keywords with OR.

Browser   A software program that translates and allows you to view HTML files.

Cache   The location where browsers keep a copy of recently visited pages in case you want to quickly review the pages. The two types of caches are a place in Random Access Memory (RAM) or a location on your hard drive. If the cache your browser uses is in RAM, then the memory is cleared when you exit the browser. If the cache your browser uses is on the hard

drive, the files will be flushed after a certain period of time, or you can delete them manually.

CC   The shorthand for Carbon Copy. The field in an e-mail message that is used to send e-mail to people who should be made aware of the information in the e-mail message but to whom the e-mail is not directly addressed. The *CC:* field works just like it would in a paper memo; however, the message is sent automatically. Both the recipient who was named in the TO: field and the people who have been CC'd will be aware of the fact the e-mail was sent to all parties.

checksum   A mathematical calculation that verifies whether the data being transferred in a packet has been corrupted. If the calculation performed when the data is received does not match the figure in the packet, then the data was garbled, and the recipient machine asks the sender to send that particular packet again.

client   The computer on your desk, from which you access information on the World Wide Web.

client–server   The model that enables communication between the client computer, your desktop system, and a server, which is a more powerful computer that responds to the client's requests. It allows the client computer to request information from the server but make use of its own processing power.

communications (COM) port   The port to which your modem connects to your computer. Also known as the serial interface.

Cookies   Text files that Web sites you visit store on your computer. The file can include your user name, the date you last visited the Web site, and any other information that the developer of the Web site wants to put into the file. When you visit the Web site again, your browser will look for a cookie file on your hard drive, and if it finds one, it will send the file to the site. The Web site then uses the information in the cookie file to tailor the information at the Web site to your preferences.

cyberspace   The communications that take place on the Internet.

data compression   The process in which the modem sending data recognizes common elements in the data and replaces the elements with shorter codes. This shortened code transfers more quickly over your modem. The receiving modem then recognizes the codes and translates them back into the original elements.

date   In an e-mail message, this field contains the date and time stamp of your message.

decoding   A method of converting encoded files back to their original form.

Directories   Catalogs or indexes of Web sites compiled by researchers whose job is to create databases. The information is organized into a hierarchy of categories from which you can narrow your search by topic.

domain   The name of a particular Internet site.

download   The act of moving information from a distant computer to your local computer.

dumb terminals   Machines that have no computing capability but rather just sit with an open connection to their server and either input to or receive information from the server.

electronic bulletin board systems (BBS)   A user-run service that allows users to communicate by posting messages.

e-mail   Electronic mail—messages that are sent and received electronically.

encoding   A method of translating complex documents into simple symbols that can be transferred using SMTP.

encryption   The process by which you scramble information in an e-mail message for security purposes.

Enhanced V.34   V-dot standard for the transmission speed of 33.6 kbps.

error control   This standard establishes a method of detecting and correcting errors during the transmission of messages over your modem.

favorites   A listing that you create to list sites you visit often or would like to quickly return to. Also known as "bookmarks."

filters   In an e-mail program, this option uses information in the header of an e-mail message to sort through mail.

Forward   In an e-mail program, this option allows you to easily forward an e-mail message you have received to another person.

FreeNets   ISPs that provide varying levels of free access to the Internet. They are often available as part of a local library or a community center, and have most likely been formed using volunteer time, community contributions, and free hardware contributions.

From   In an e-mail message, this field contains the e-mail address of the person or organization from whom the e-mail was sent. This field may differ from the "Sender" field of an e-mail message if you are receiving mail from a mailing list.

gateway   A computer whose basic job is to search through all the incoming messages on a network for items that may be harmful to the network.

Gopher   A text-based Internet protocol that allows people to view documents in a menu-driven environment.

Header   This item comes at the beginning of an e-mail message and announces information such as who the message is for, who the message is from, and what the subject of the message is.

helper applications   Software applications that are completely separate programs from the browser but that will open upon request by the browser.

history list   A listing created by your browser of the last Web pages visited.

hits   The number of matches a search engine returns to you based on your search.

home page   The main or introductory World Wide Web page for a site.

host-remote   An older configuration in which the host computer does all the processing and the remote terminal simply sees the results.

hypermedia   The clickable multimedia links (including video and audio clips) in an HTML or World Wide Web document that will transfer you to a linked file.

hypertext   A word or phrase that has the address of another document embedded in it. When you click on the hot word, you are transferred to the linked document.

HyperText Transfer Protocol (HTTP)   The protocol that enables the transfer of the request and the subsequent transfer of the linked document in a World Wide Web interaction.

inbox   In an e-mail program, the location where new e-mail arrives.

Index   *See Directories.*

Internet backbone   The high-speed network that makes up the infrastructure of the Internet.

Internet Message Access Protocol (IMAP)   A protocol that downloads mail from the mail server to your personal computer. This protocol is more advanced than POP because, rather than just taking all your mail off the server like POP does, IMAP allows you to read through your messages and choose which messages you want to download to your computer and which messages you want to leave on the server. Furthermore, it will even allow you to download selected parts of messages rather than entire messages.

Internet service providers   Entities that provide access to the Internet. Also called ISPs.

Keywords   Words typed into the query box that the search tool matches in the database.

listprocessor   An automated software program that distributes your message to a large group of people via e-mail. Also known as a mailing list or listserver.

listserver   An automated software program that distributes your message to a large group of people via e-mail. Also known as a mailing list or listprocessor.

mailing list   An automated software program that distributes your message to a large group of people via e-mail. Also known as a listprocessor or listserver.

MIME (Multipurpose Internet Multimedia Extensions)   The most common method of encoding nontext files.

nested folder system   In an e-mail program, this option allows you to create a hierarchy of folders or subfolders to organize your e-mail messages. For example, if you are working on several projects, you might want to have a folder for correspondence that relates to each project. Because the volume of e-mail for any project could be quite large, you can then create subfolders for each project.

newbies   People who are new to using the Internet.

newsgroups   Discussion groups that use the NNTP protocol to post messages to news servers.

nicknames   In an e-mail program, an option that allows you to associate a short nickname with an e-mail address. When you need to send an e-mail to this e-mail address, you can invoke it by using the nickname.

NSFNET   National Science Foundation Network.

Online service providers   Entities that provide access to the Internet along with extra services. Their extra services including online sports information, stock market information, interactive games, and encyclopedic information will have to be updated to follow the standards of the Internet.

packet-switching   The process whereby packets are transferred over the Internet. Packets that contain the address of the recipient and the sender travel the Internet separately over different paths and are reassembled by the recipient. If a packet is lost or becomes garbled, then the recipient asks for that packet to be re-sent.

passphrase   This item is similar to a password except that it consists of an entire phrase rather than just one word.

password   A word that is used as part of a login for security purposes.

Personal Computer Memory Card International Association (PCMCIA)   The regulatory body that creates the standards for all implementations of PC cards.

plug-ins   Software applications that expand a browser's basic capabilities by actually becoming extensions of the browser itself.

Post Office Protocol (POP)   A protocol that downloads mail from the mail server to your personal computer.

priority settings   In an e-mail program, an option that allows the sender to emphasize how important the message is by setting the message as high or low priority.

private key   This item is used in security systems along with public keys to ensure only you can

read your e-mail. You use this key to verify the private key and to unlock your messages.

Program launch   In an e-mail program, this option allows you to open the program to which a file is associated by simply clicking on a highlighted link.

proprietary   Information or software that is specific to one or a few entities. In terms of proprietary software, this term refers to special software that is required to access certain services or information. You cannot access these services or information without the special software.

protocol   A set of standards.

public key   This item is used in security systems along with private keys to ensure only you can read your e-mail. Each person who sends you e-mail must attach your public key to the message.

query box   The text box provided by the search site into which you type the keyword for which you want to search.

Redirect   In an e-mail program, this option allows you to easily forward an e-mail message you have received to another person while making sure that the other person realizes the e-mail message originally came from someone else.

redundancy   Repeat connections to access points that stabilize the connection to the Internet because they allow information to be rerouted past areas where the connections are down.

Reply   In an e-mail program, this option allows you to reply easily to the person who has sent you an e-mail message.

Reply All   In an e-mail program, this option allows you to reply easily to all the people who were listed as recipients to the e-mail that you have received.

Reply-To   In an e-mail message, this field contains the e-mail address of the person or organization to which your message will be sent if you click the Reply button in your e-mail program.

Robots   Software used by search engines that visit Web sites, index all the Web pages, and put the information into databases.

routers   Computers on the Internet that forward packets to their destination.

search engines   The second main category of search tools. Search engines search for the keyword or words you type into the query box and find documents that contain the words. They use spiders, robots, and webcrawlers to search through Web pages and record keywords found on those Web pages in databases.

search tool   Software designed to help you find information on the World Wide Web.

Sender   In an e-mail message, this field contains the e-mail address of the person or organization from whom the e-mail was sent. This field may differ from the From field of an e-mail message if you are receiving mail from a mailing list.

serial interface The port to which your modem connects to your computer. Also known as the communications or COM port.

Set-top Hardware and software that allow you to access the Internet over your television system.

Signatures In an e-mail program, this option allows the sender to include his or her contact information automatically at the end of an e-mail message.

Simple Mail Transfer Protocol (SMTP) The protocol built on top of TCP/IP whose sole purpose is to get e-mail messages from the sender's machine to the receiver's mail server.

snail mail Regular U.S. Postal Service mail.

spelling checkers In an e-mail program, this option allows you to check your message manually for spelling errors.

Spiders Software used by search engines that visit Web sites, index all the Web pages, and put the information into databases.

Subject In an e-mail message, this field contains a short summary of what is contained in the message.

TCP/IP Transmission Control Protocol/Internet Protocol. The fundamental suite of protocols that determine how information is sent over the Internet.

To In an e-mail message, this field contains the e-mail address of the person to whom you are sending the message.

transmission speed The speed at which your modem transfers files. It is most commonly measured in bits per second (bps) or kilobits per second (kbps).

Uniform Resource Locator (URL) The address of a World Wide Web document.

UNIX A powerful operating system on which many Web servers reside.

upload The act of moving information from your local computer to a distant computer.

UserID The name with which you log on to the Internet for security purposes.

UUENCODE A method of encoding nontext files. Mostly used by UNIX systems.

V.22bis V-dot standard for the transmission speed of 2400 bps.

V.32 V-dot standard for the transmission speed of 9600 bps.

V.32bis V-dot standard for the transmission speed of 14.4 kbps.

V.34 V-dot standard for the transmission speed of 28.8 kbps.

V.42 V-dot standard for error correction.

V.42bis V-dot standard for data compression.

virtual communities Groups of people who have common interests, share communication, and feel a sense of community with others who are online.

Web server The computer that contains HTML documents that people access to view World Wide Web pages.

webcrawlers Software used by search engines that visit Web sites, index all the Web pages, and put the information into databases.

World Wide Web World Wide Web—linked documents that reside on computers all over the world.

Index